CLONE WARS

ADVENTURES

VOLUME 6

designer
Joshua Elliott

assistant editor
Dave Marshall

editor
Jeremy Barlow

publisher
Mike Richardson

special thanks to Sue Rostoni, Leland Chee,
and Amy Gary at Lucas Licensing

talk about this book online at: *www.darkhorse.com/community/boards*

The events in this story take place
just before and during the events in
Star Wars: Episode III *Revenge of the Sith*

Advertising Sales: (503) 652-8815 x370
Comic Shop Locator Service: (888) 266-4226
www.darkhorse.com
www.starwars.com

STAR WARS: CLONE WARS ADVENTURES Volume 6, August 2006. Published
by Dark Horse Comics, Inc., 10956 SE Main Street, Milwaukie, OR 97222. Star Wars
©2006 Lucasfilm Ltd. & ™. All rights reserved. Used under authorization. Text and
illustrations for Star Wars are © 2006 Lucasfilm Ltd. Dark Horse Comics® and the
Dark Horse logo are trademarks of Dark Horse Comics, Inc., registered in various
categories and countries. All rights reserved.

STAR WARS

CLONE WARS
ADVENTURES
VOLUME 6

IT TAKES A THIEF
script and art **The Fillbach Brothers**
colors **Ronda Pattison**

THE DROP
script **Mike Kennedy**
art **Stewart McKenney**
colors **Ronda Pattison**

TO THE VANISHING POINT
script and art **The Fillbach Brothers**
colors **Ronda Pattison**

MEANS AND ENDS
script **Haden Blackman**
art **Rick Lacy**
colors **Dan Jackson**

lettering
Michael David Thomas

cover
The Fillbach Brothers and Dan Jackson

Dark Horse Books™

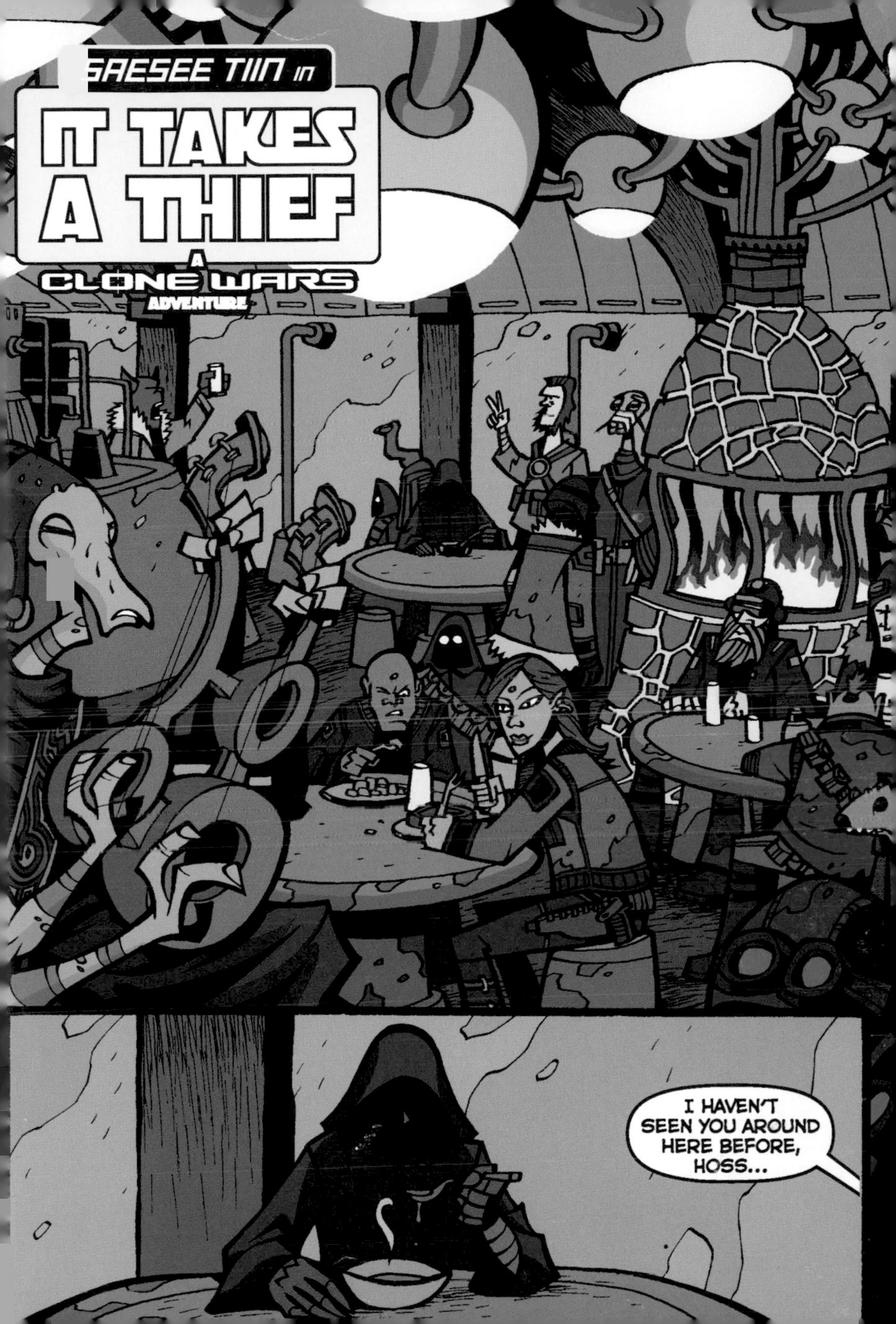
SAESEE TIIN in
IT TAKES A THIEF
A CLONE WARS ADVENTURE
I HAVEN'T SEEN YOU AROUND HERE BEFORE, HOSS...

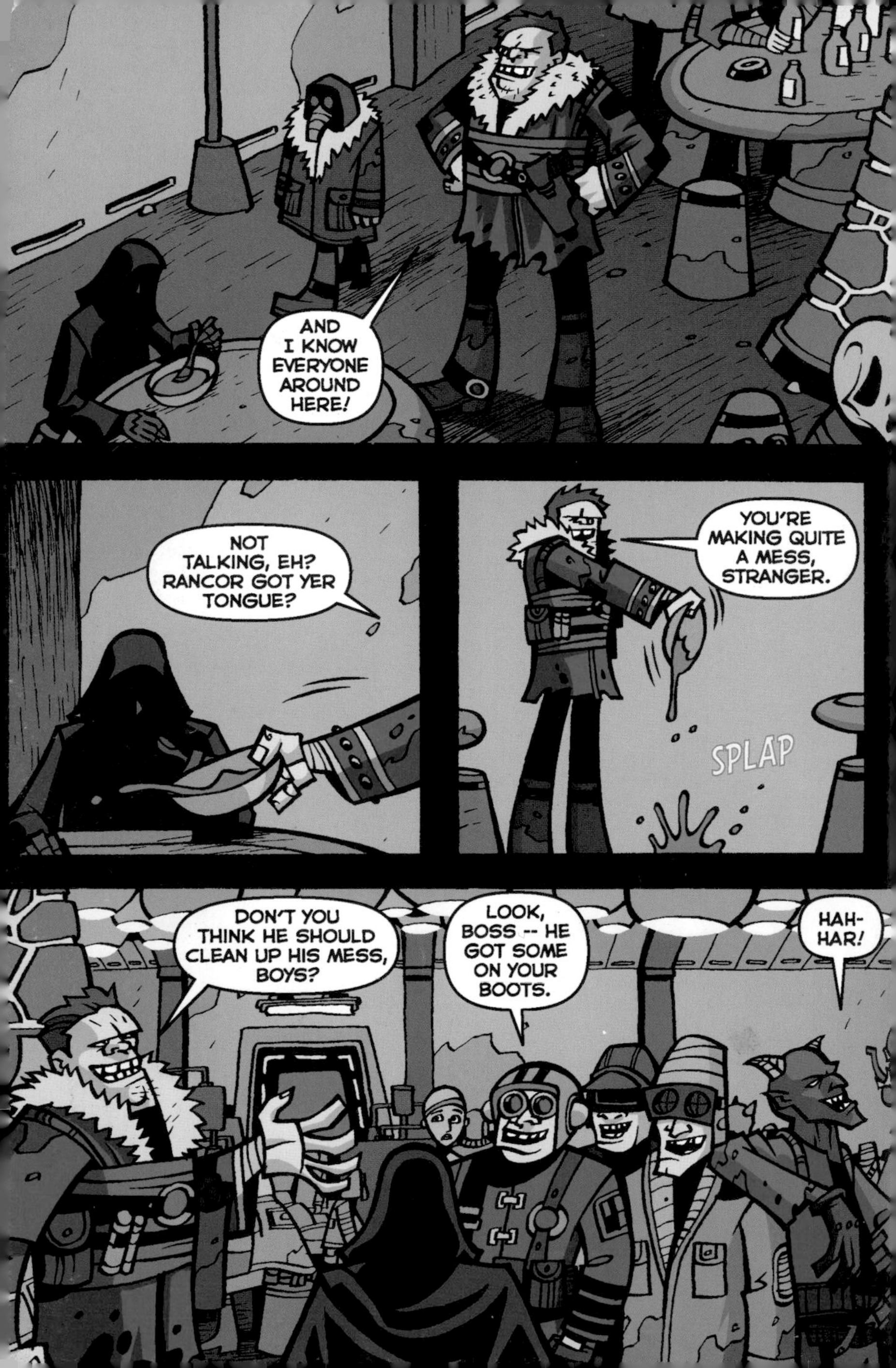
AND I KNOW EVERYONE AROUND HERE!
NOT TALKING, EH? RANCOR GOT YER TONGUE?
YOU'RE MAKING QUITE A MESS, STRANGER.
SPLAP
DON'T YOU THINK HE SHOULD CLEAN UP HIS MESS, BOYS?
LOOK, BOSS -- HE GOT SOME ON YOUR BOOTS.
HAH-HAR!

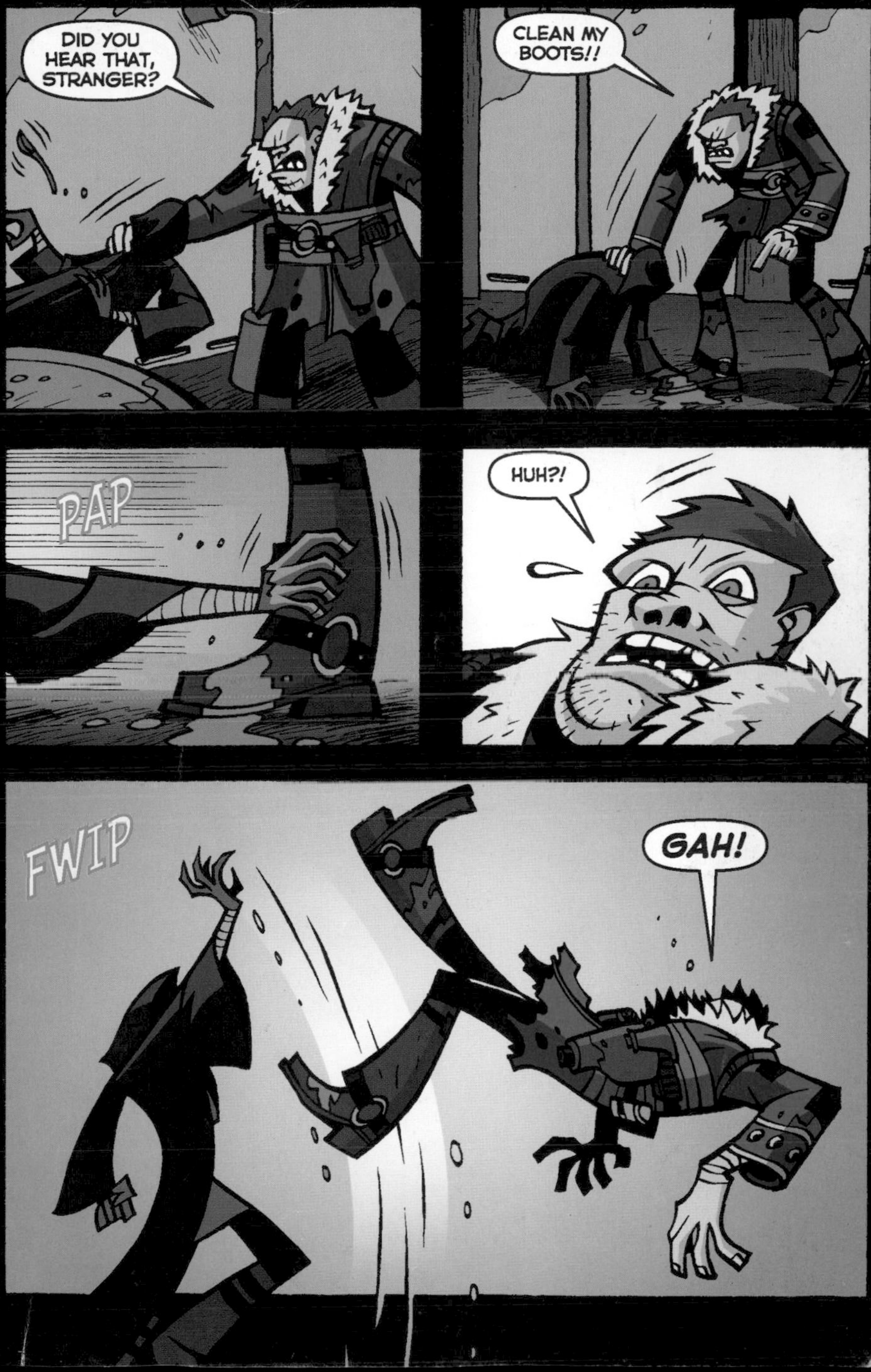
DID YOU HEAR THAT, STRANGER?
CLEAN MY BOOTS!!
PAP
HUH?!
FWIP
GAH!

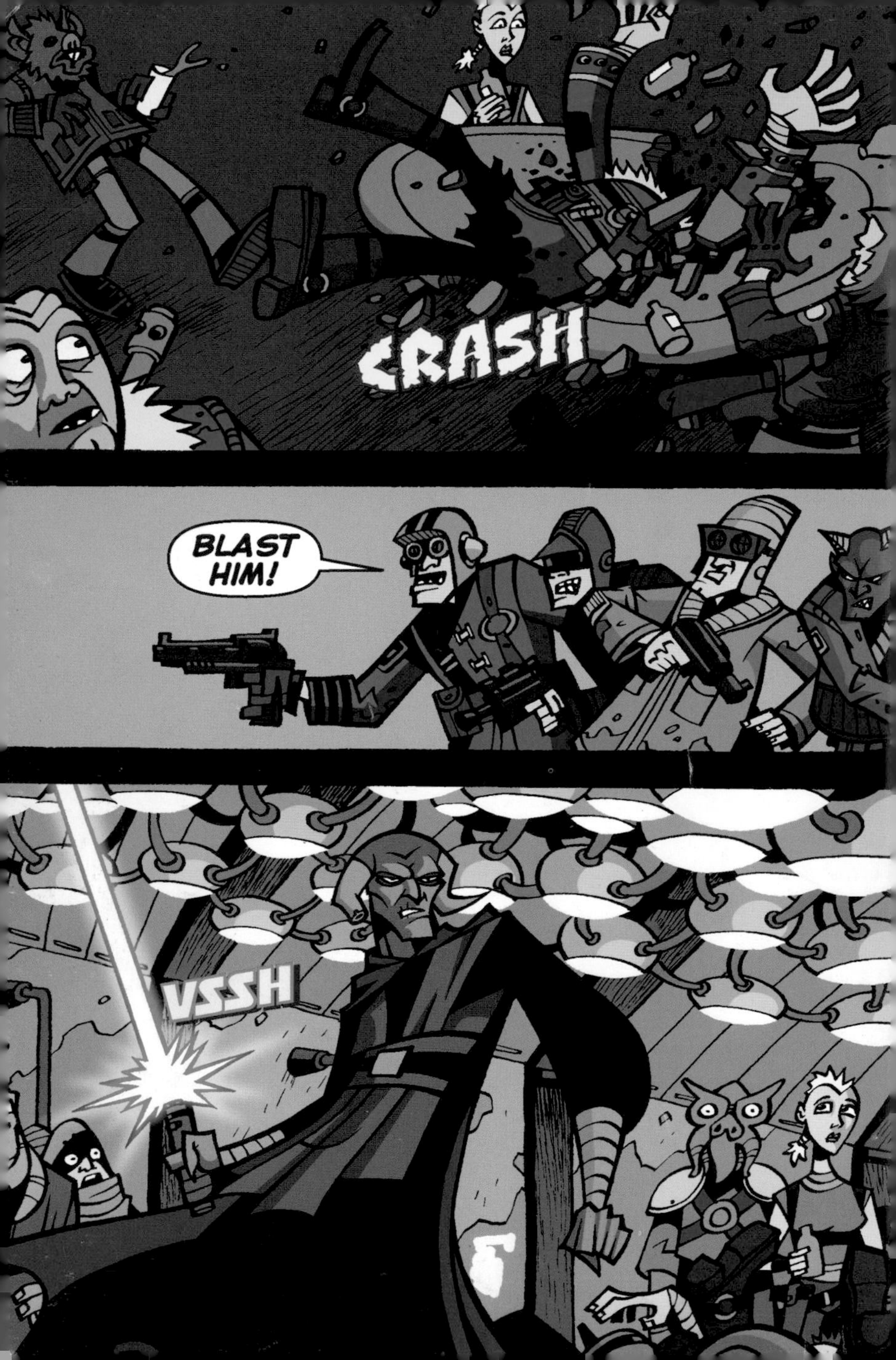
CRASH
BLAST HIM!
VSSH

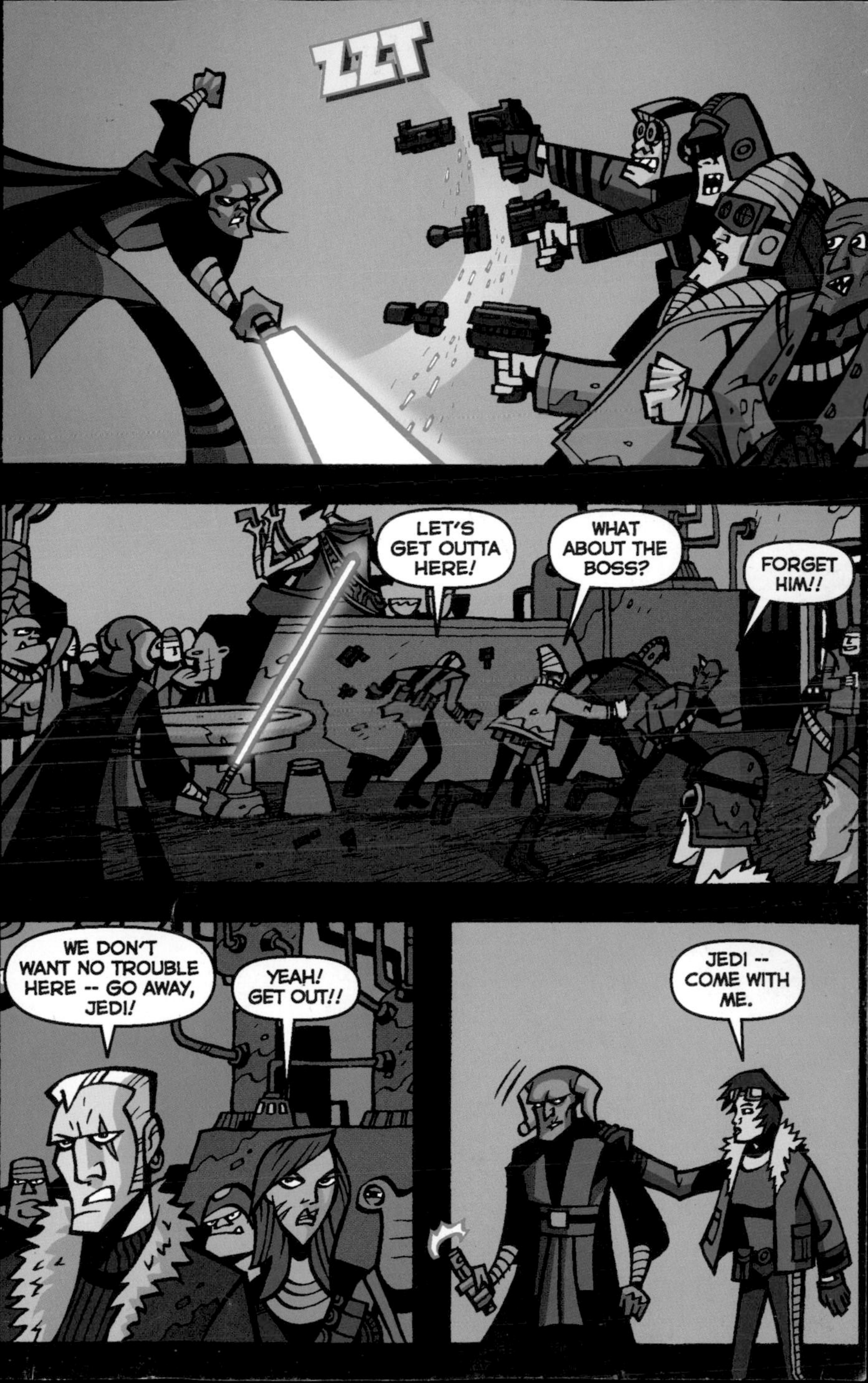
ZZT
LET'S GET OUTTA HERE!
WHAT ABOUT THE BOSS?
FORGET HIM!!
WE DON'T WANT NO TROUBLE HERE -- GO AWAY, JEDI!
YEAH! GET OUT!!
JEDI -- COME WITH ME.

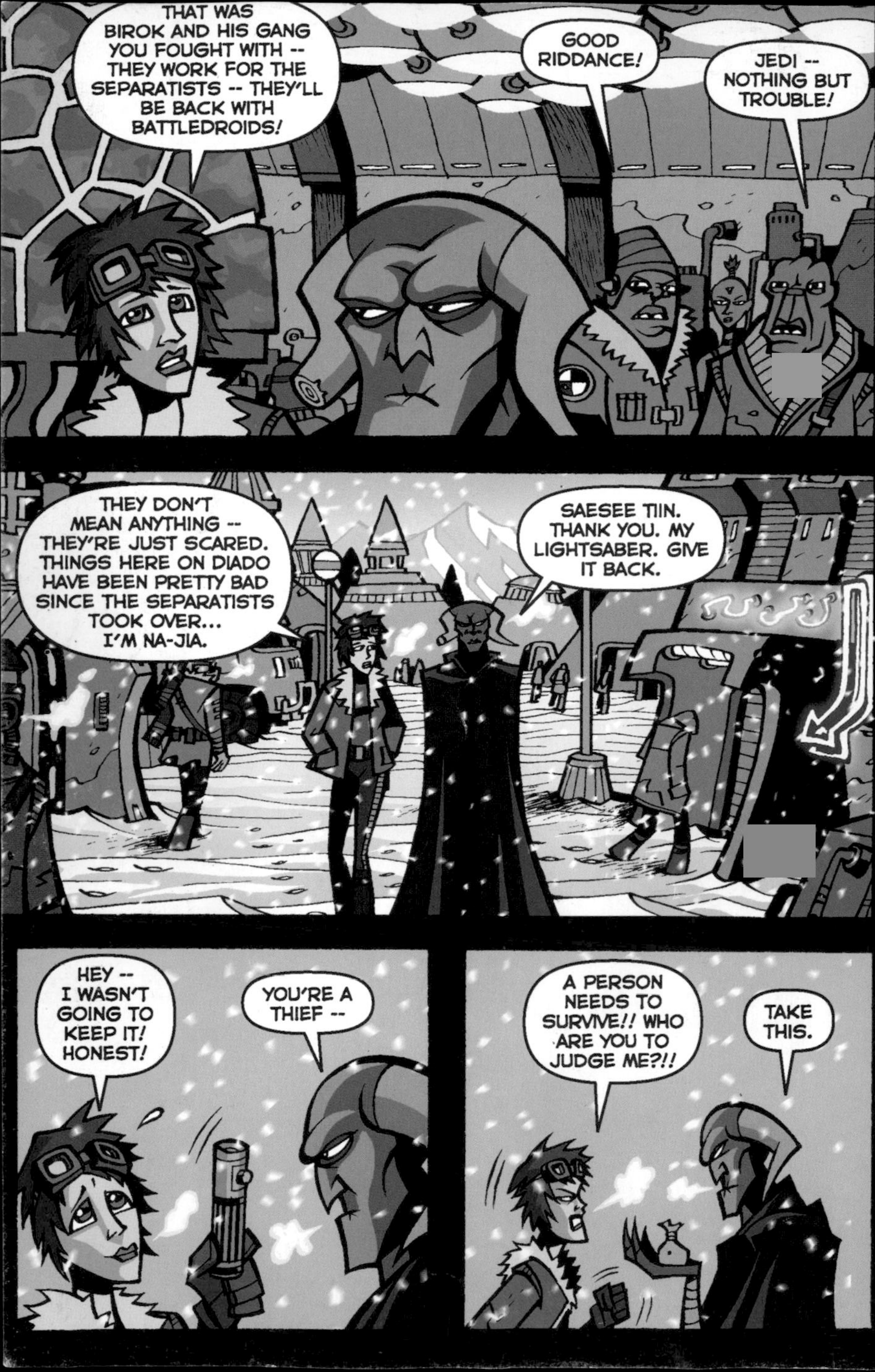
THAT WAS BIROK AND HIS GANG YOU FOUGHT WITH -- THEY WORK FOR THE SEPARATISTS -- THEY'LL BE BACK WITH BATTLEDROIDS!
GOOD RIDDANCE!
JEDI -- NOTHING BUT TROUBLE!
THEY DON'T MEAN ANYTHING -- THEY'RE JUST SCARED. THINGS HERE ON DIADO HAVE BEEN PRETTY BAD SINCE THE SEPARATISTS TOOK OVER... I'M NA-JIA.
SAESEE TIIN. THANK YOU. MY LIGHTSABER. GIVE IT BACK.
HEY -- I WASN'T GOING TO KEEP IT! HONEST!
YOU'RE A THIEF --
A PERSON NEEDS TO SURVIVE!! WHO ARE YOU TO JUDGE ME?!!
TAKE THIS.

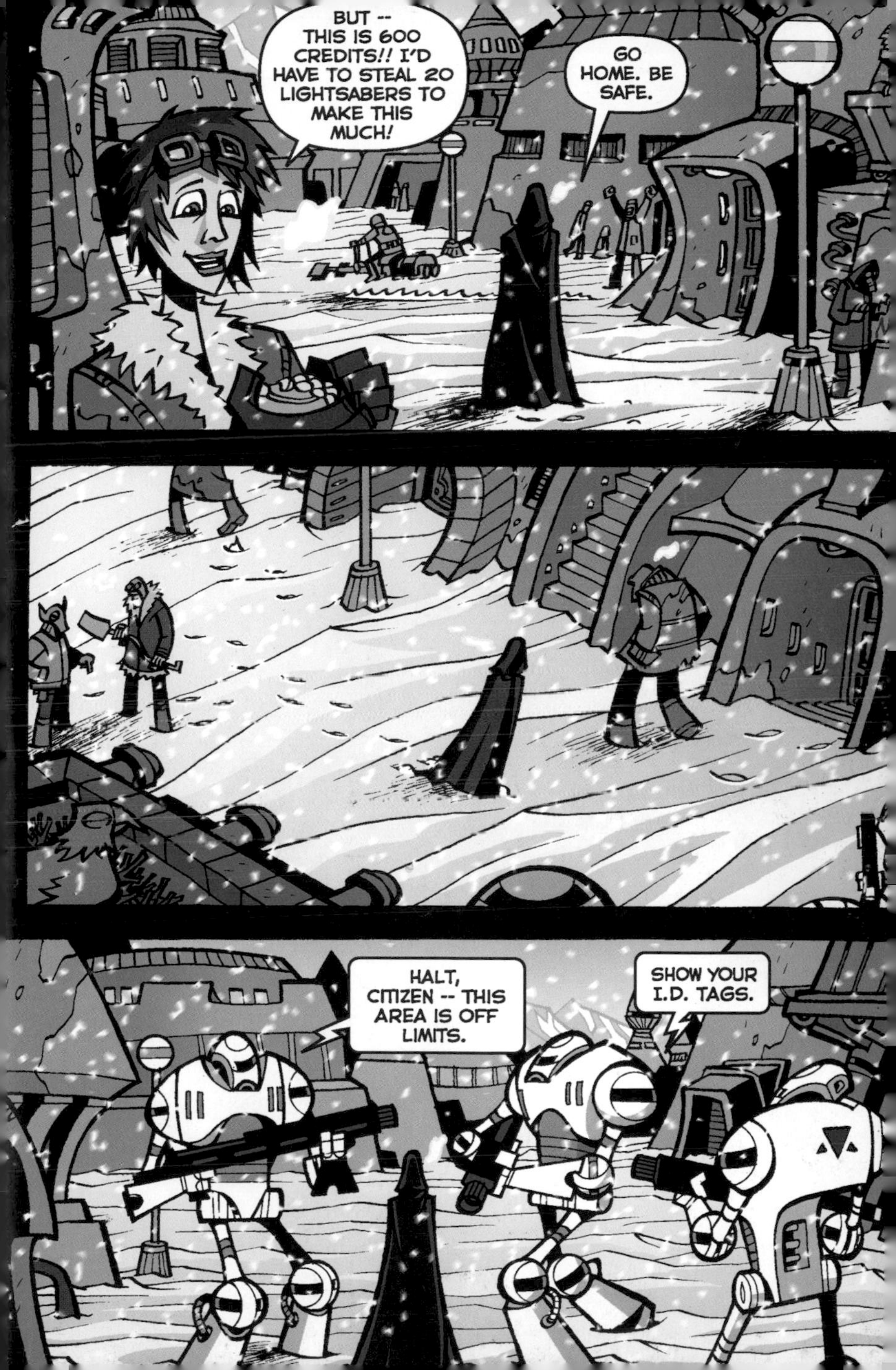
BUT -- THIS IS 600 CREDITS!! I'D HAVE TO STEAL 20 LIGHTSABERS TO MAKE THIS MUCH!
GO HOME. BE SAFE.
HALT, CITIZEN -- THIS AREA IS OFF LIMITS.
SHOW YOUR I.D. TAGS.

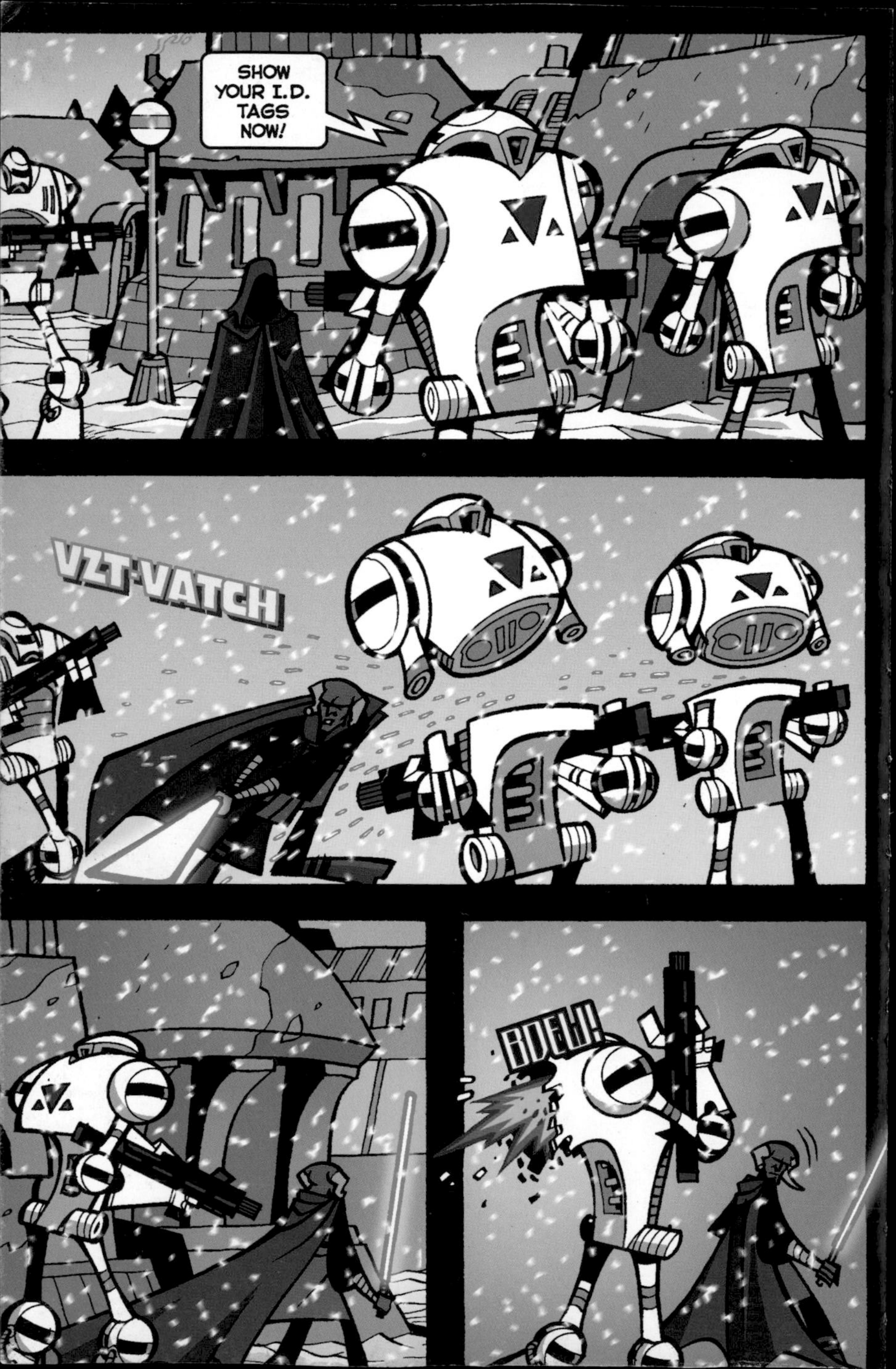
SHOW YOUR I.D. TAGS NOW!
VZT-VATCH
BDEW!

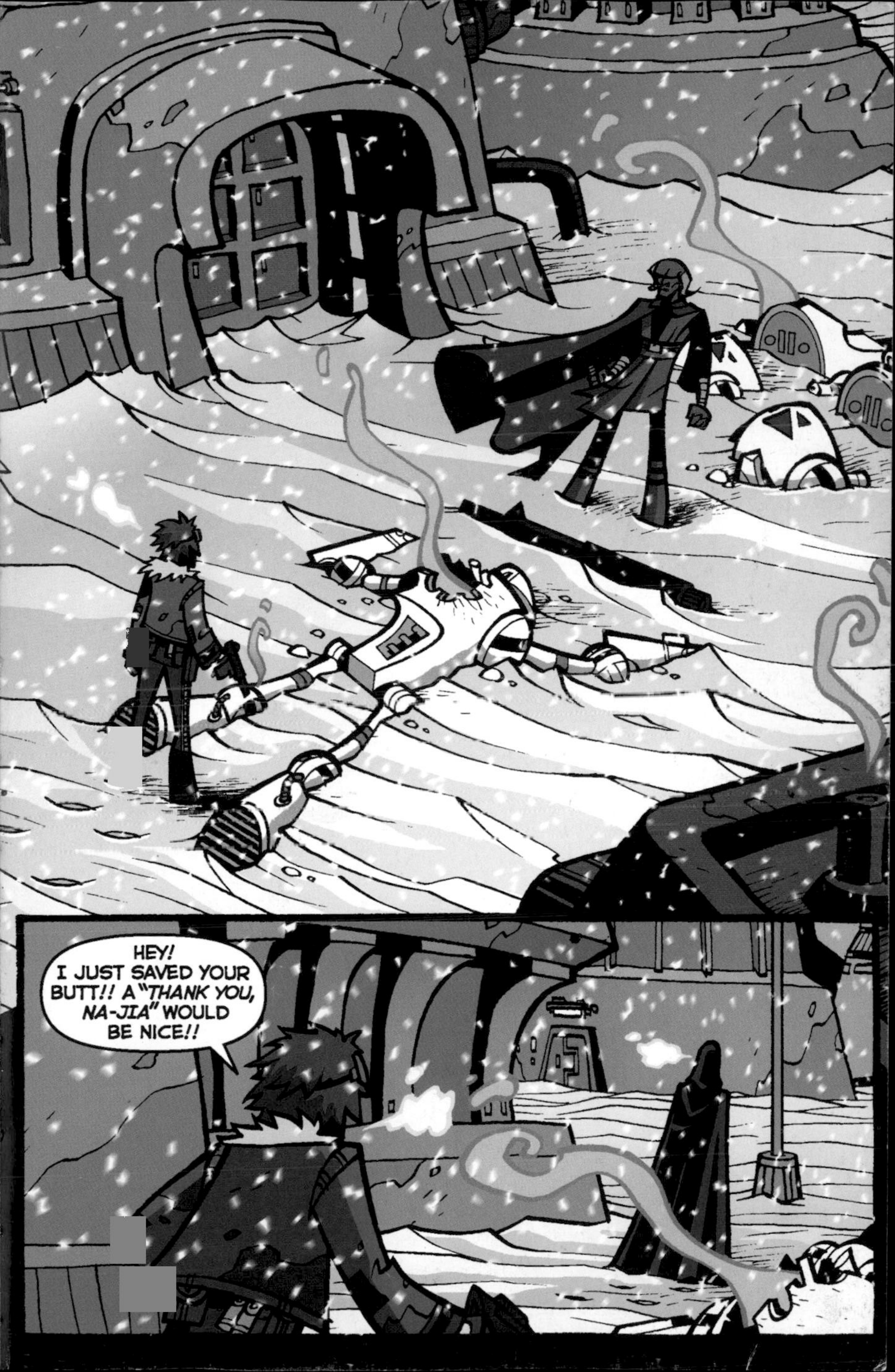
HEY! I JUST SAVED YOUR BUTT!! A "THANK YOU, NA-JIA" WOULD BE NICE!!

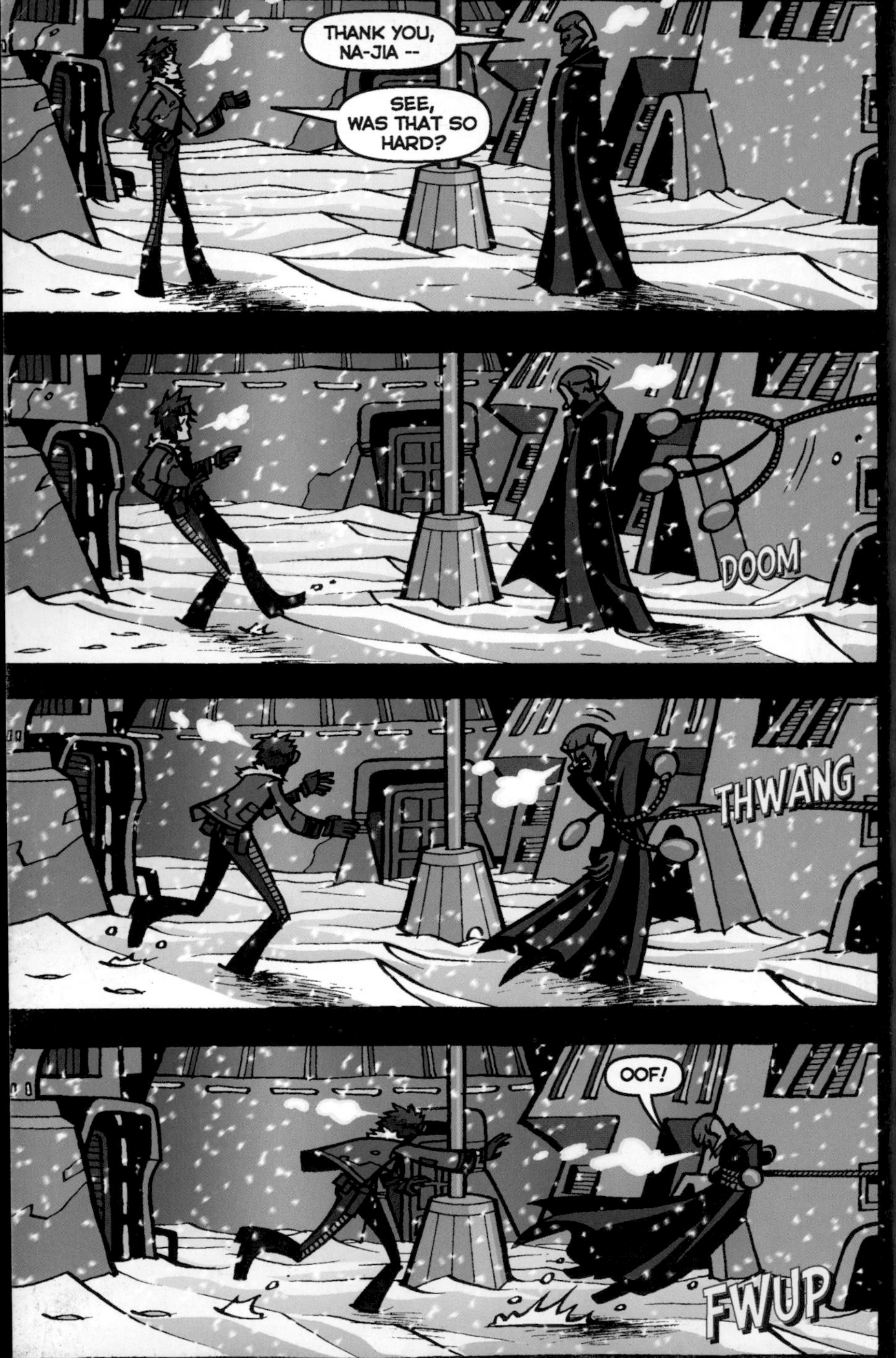
THANK YOU, NA-JIA --
SEE, WAS THAT SO HARD?
DOOM
THWANG
OOF!
FWUP

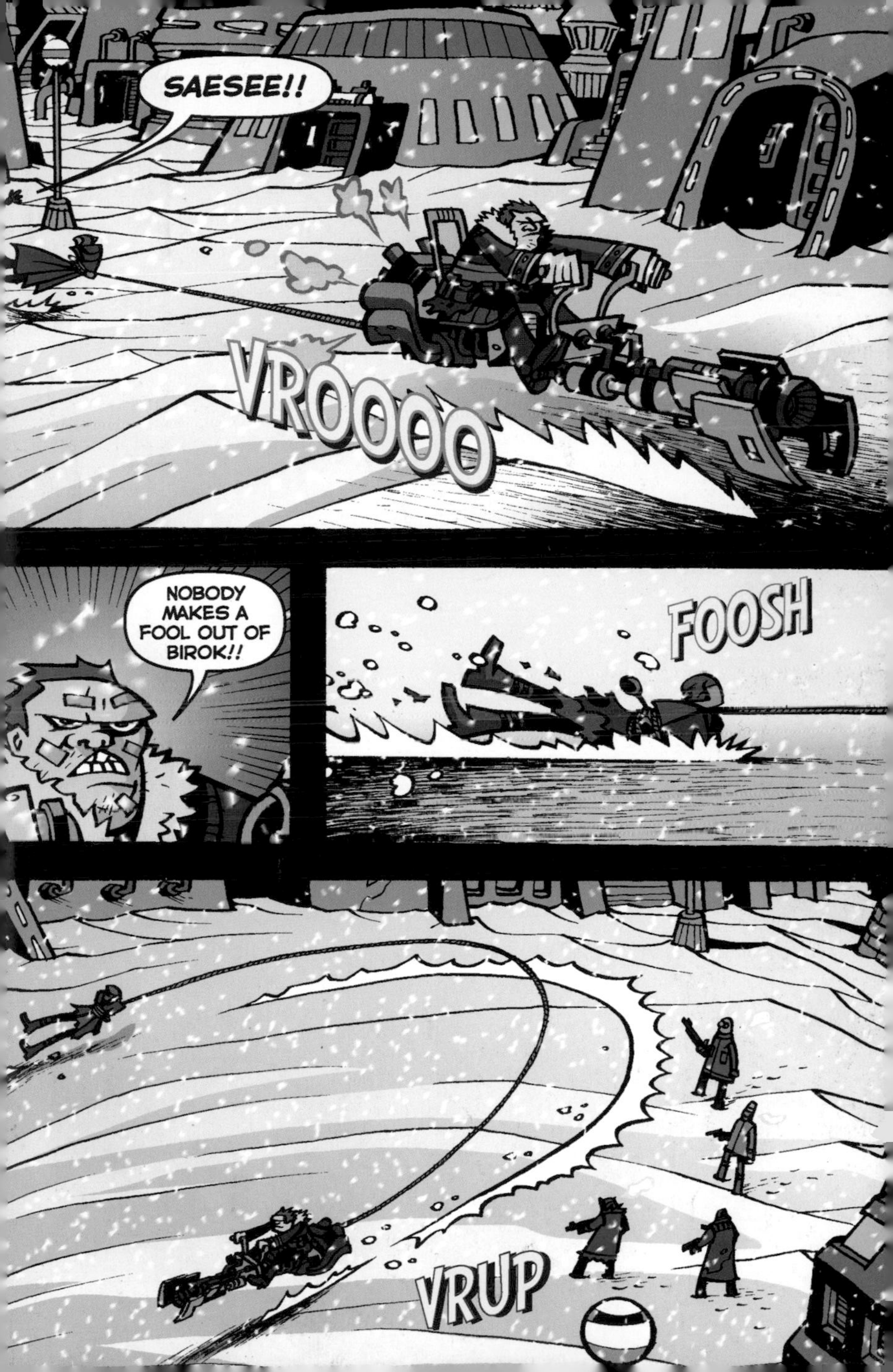
SAESEE!!
VROOOO
NOBODY MAKES A FOOL OUT OF BIROK!!
FOOSH
VRUP

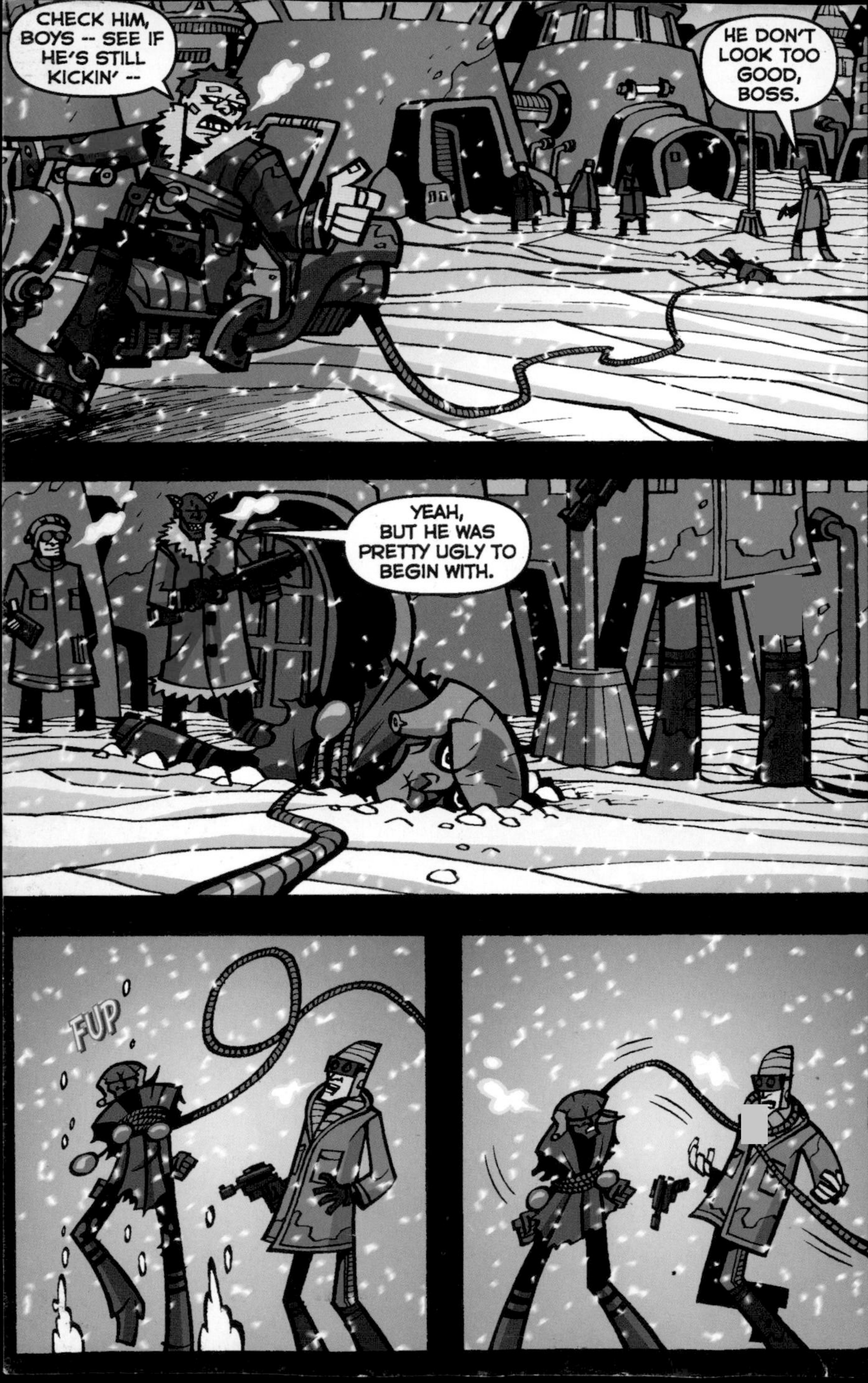
CHECK HIM, BOYS -- SEE IF HE'S STILL KICKIN' --
HE DON'T LOOK TOO GOOD, BOSS.
YEAH, BUT HE WAS PRETTY UGLY TO BEGIN WITH.
FUP

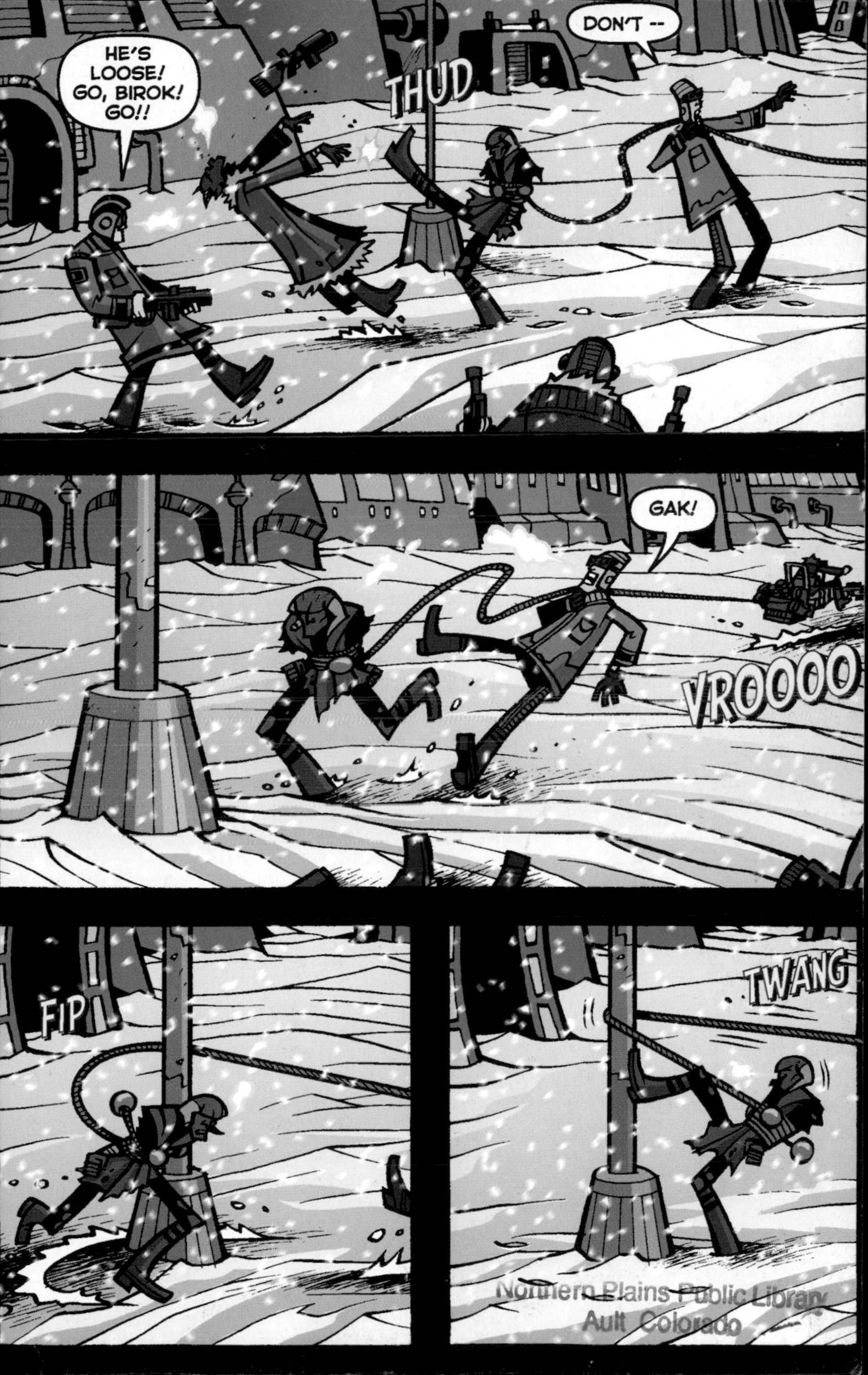
HE'S LOOSE! GO, BIROK! GO!!
THUD
DON'T --
GAK!
VROOOO
FIP
TWANG

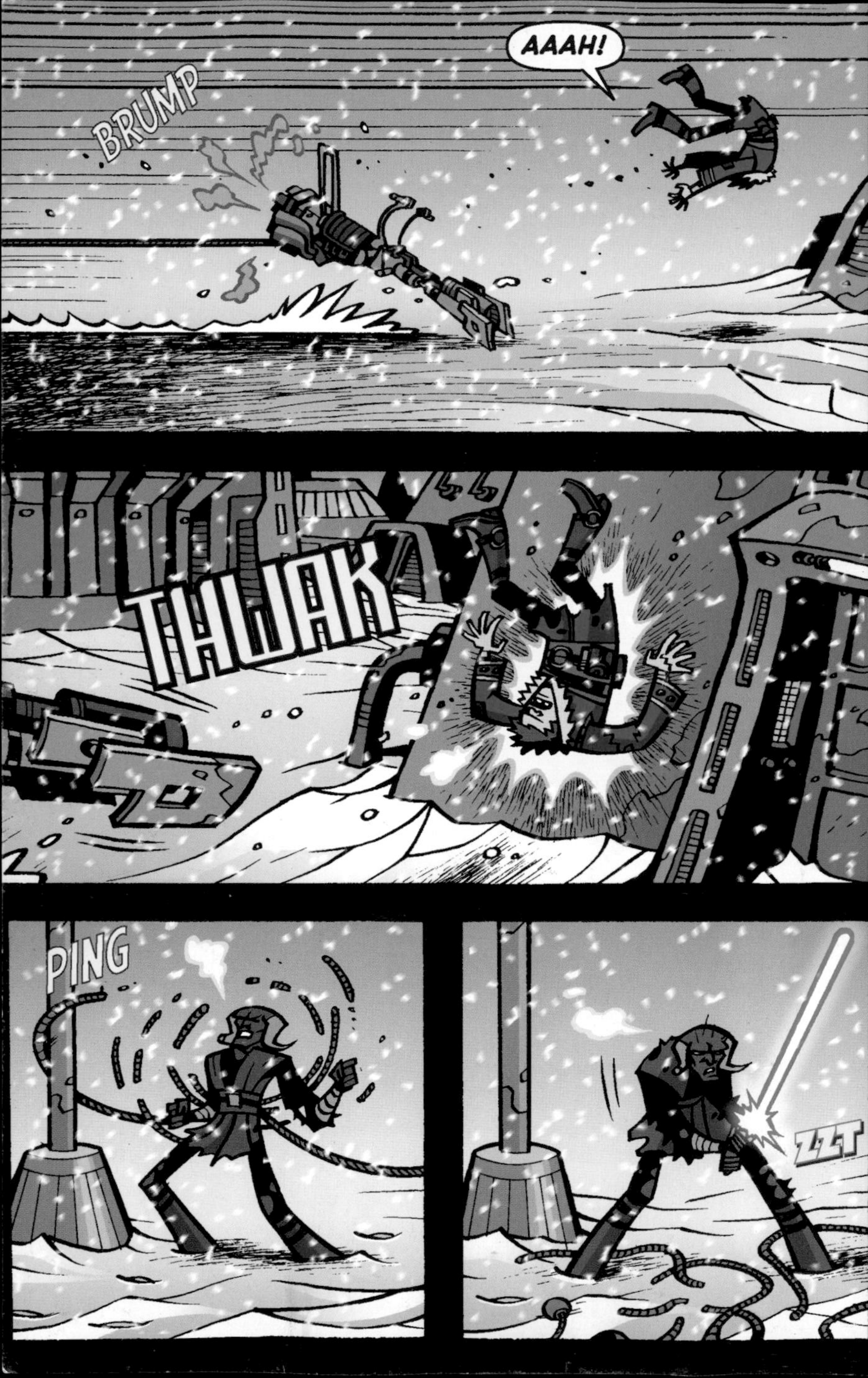
AAAH!
BRUMP
THWAK
PING
ZZT

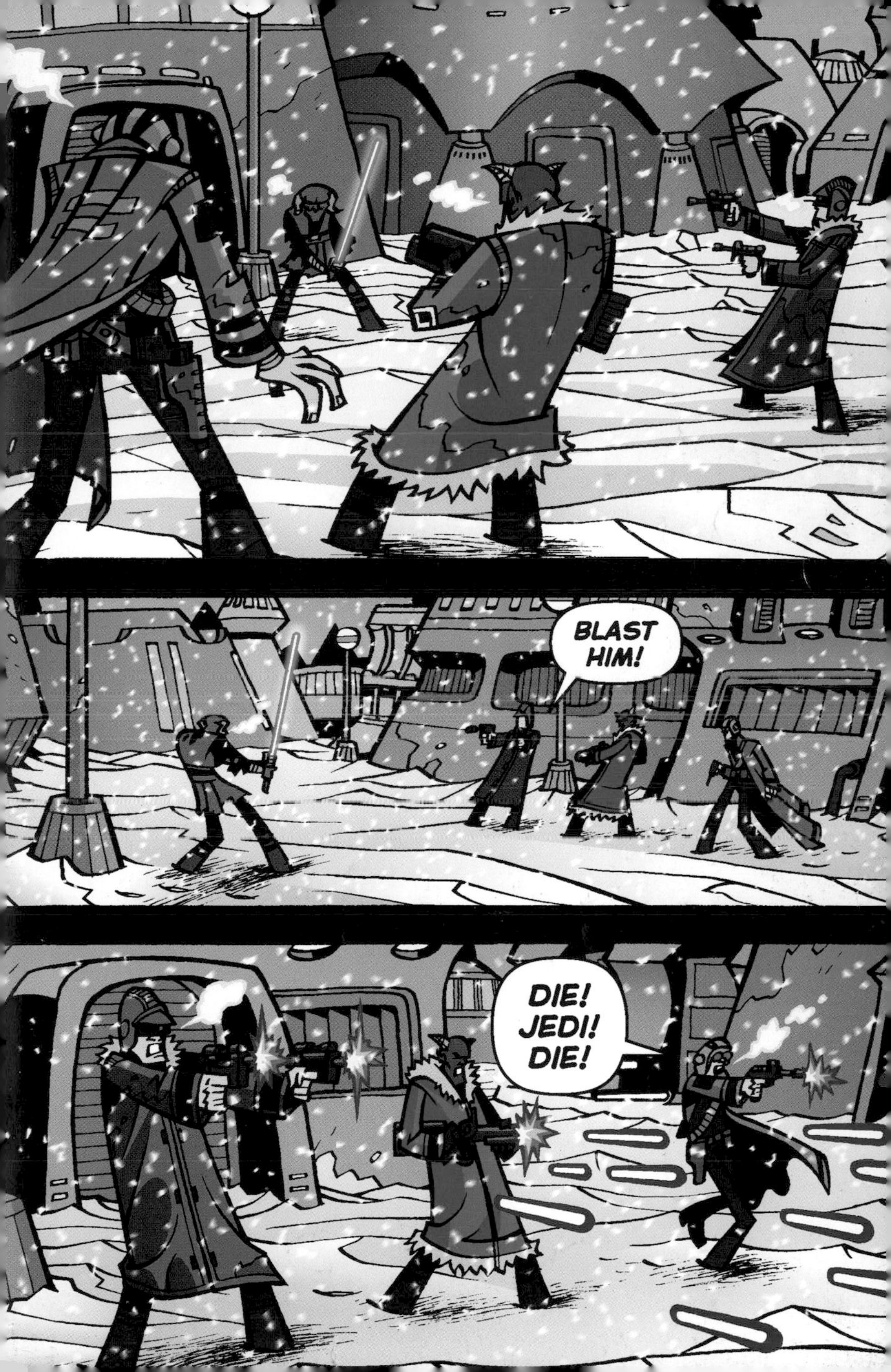
BLAST HIM!
DIE! JEDI! DIE!

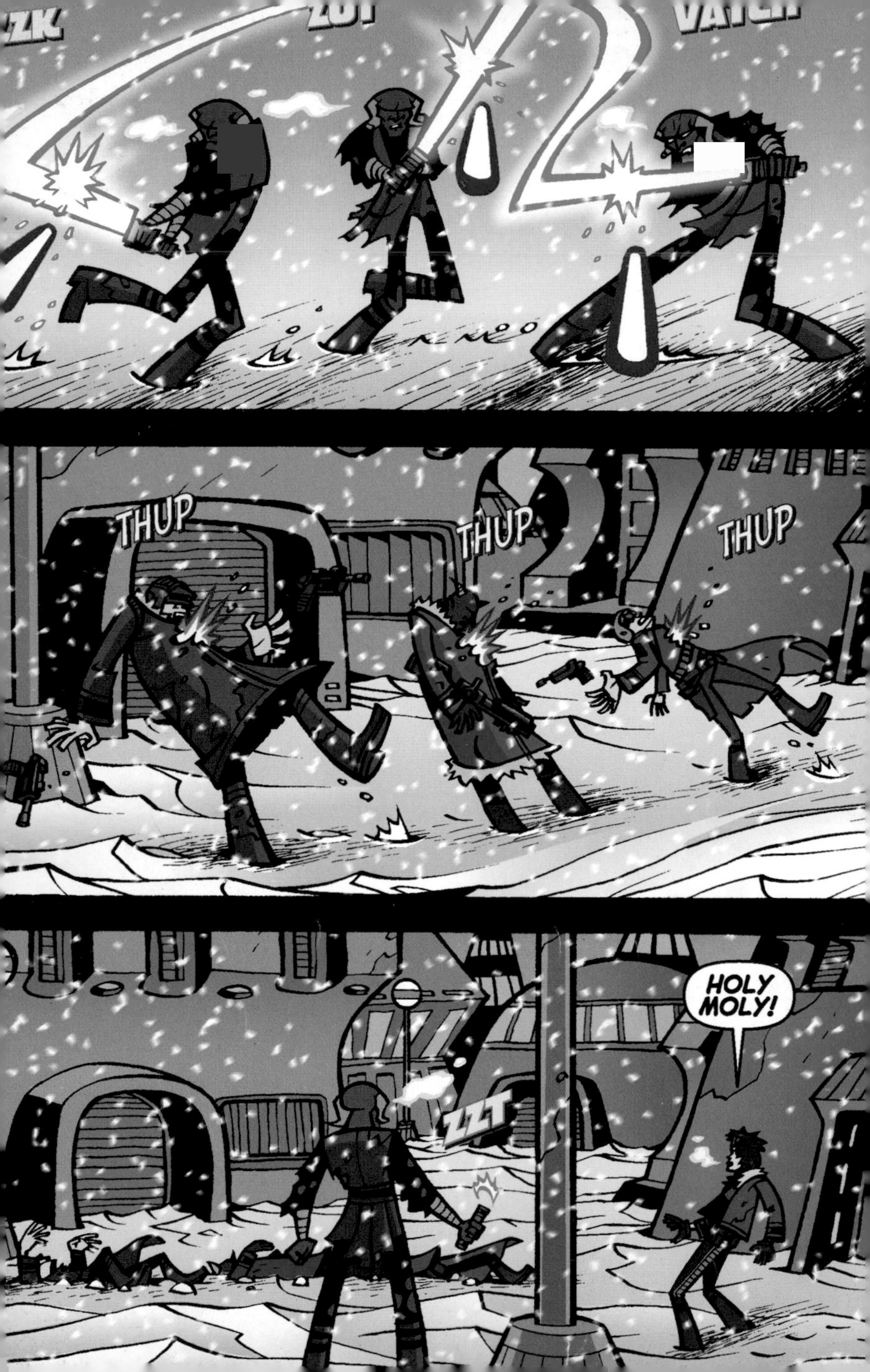
THUP
THUP
THUP
ZZT
HOLY MOLY!

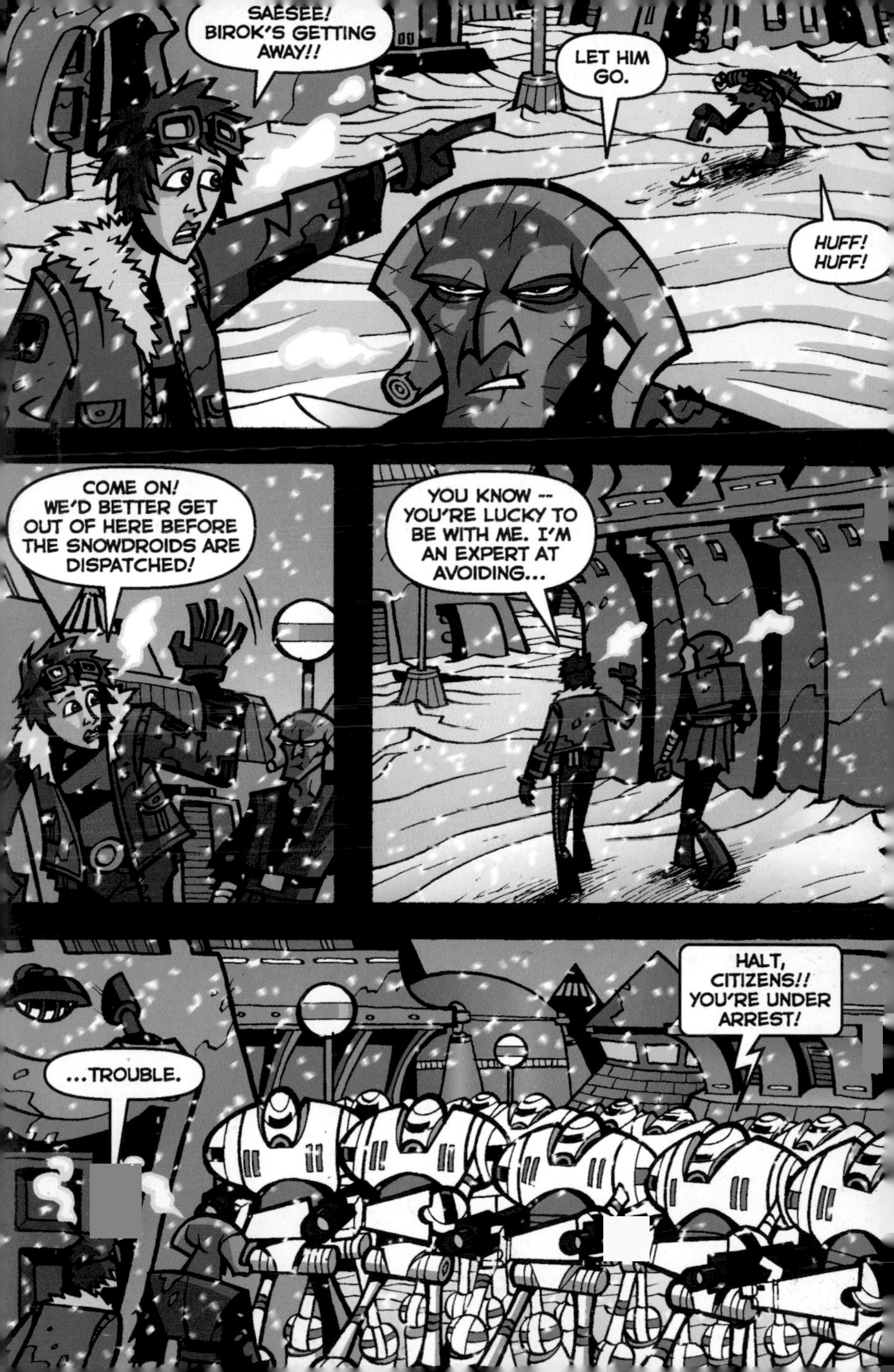
SAESEE! BIROK'S GETTING AWAY!!
LET HIM GO.
HUFF! HUFF!
COME ON! WE'D BETTER GET OUT OF HERE BEFORE THE SNOWDROIDS ARE DISPATCHED!
YOU KNOW -- YOU'RE LUCKY TO BE WITH ME. I'M AN EXPERT AT AVOIDING...
...TROUBLE.
HALT, CITIZENS!! YOU'RE UNDER ARREST!

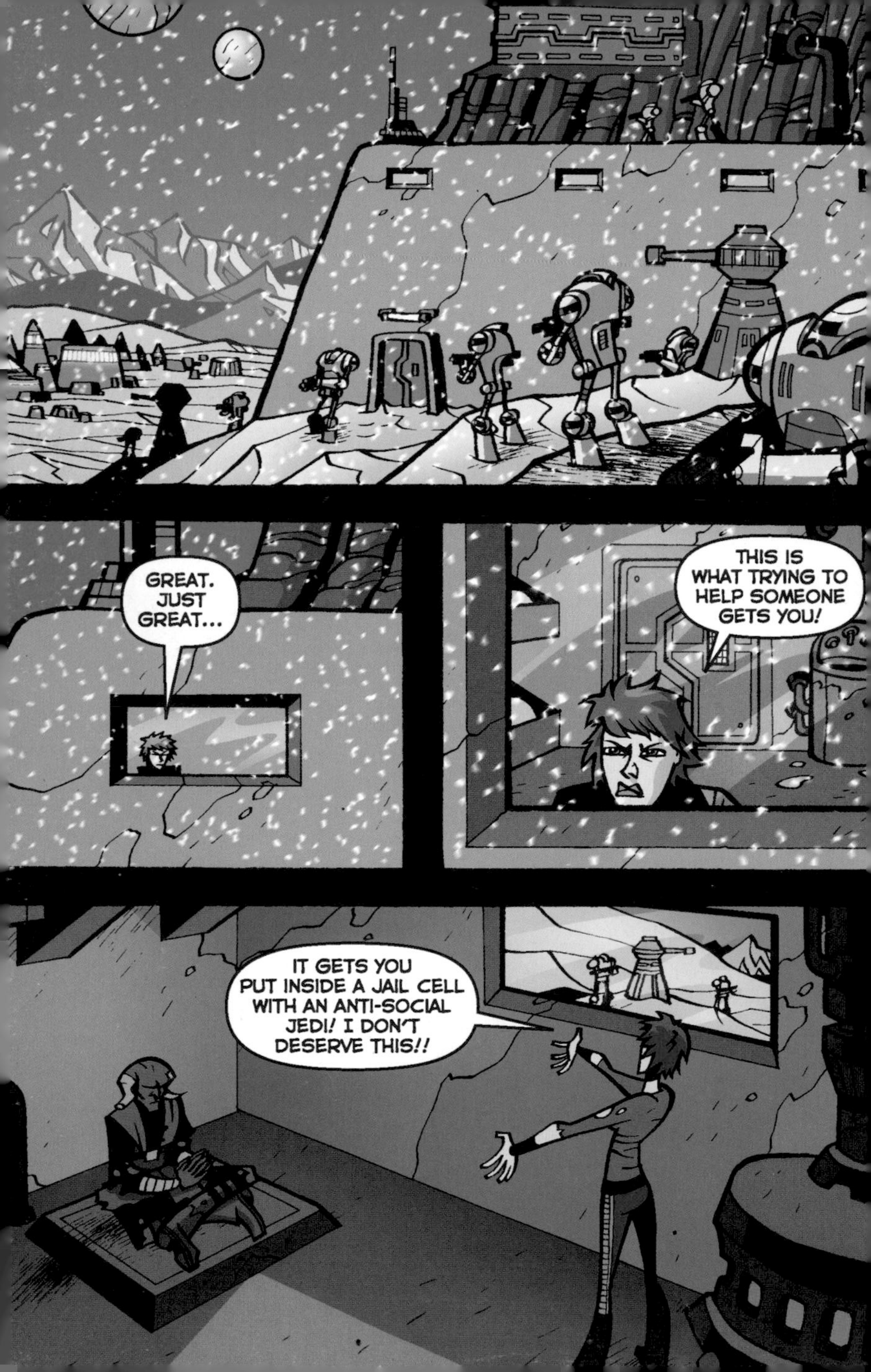
GREAT. JUST GREAT...
THIS IS WHAT TRYING TO HELP SOMEONE GETS YOU!
IT GETS YOU PUT INSIDE A JAIL CELL WITH AN ANTI-SOCIAL JEDI! I DON'T DESERVE THIS!!

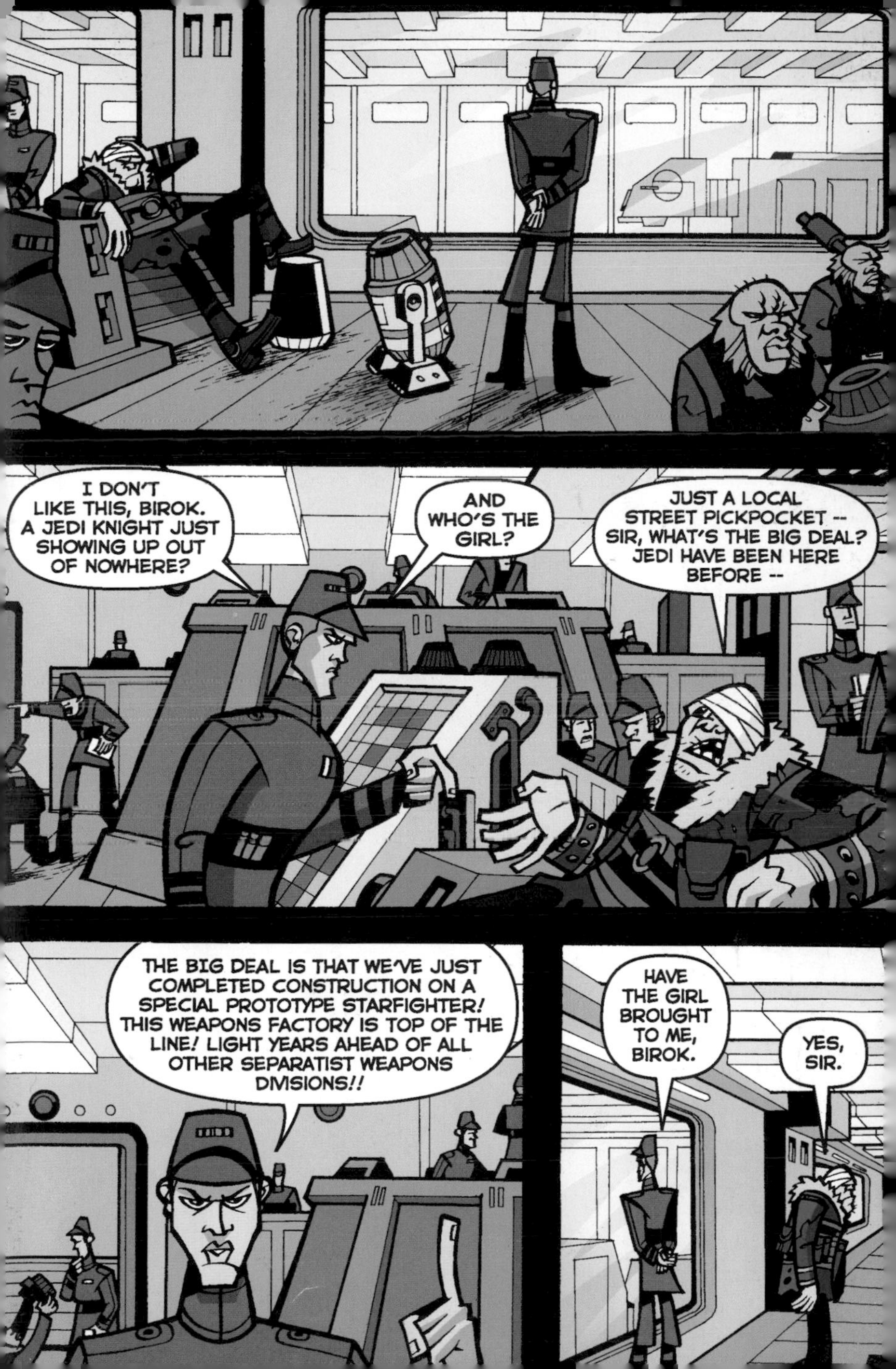
I DON'T LIKE THIS, BIROK. A JEDI KNIGHT JUST SHOWING UP OUT OF NOWHERE?
AND WHO'S THE GIRL?
JUST A LOCAL STREET PICKPOCKET -- SIR, WHAT'S THE BIG DEAL? JEDI HAVE BEEN HERE BEFORE --
THE BIG DEAL IS THAT WE'VE JUST COMPLETED CONSTRUCTION ON A SPECIAL PROTOTYPE STARFIGHTER! THIS WEAPONS FACTORY IS TOP OF THE LINE! LIGHT YEARS AHEAD OF ALL OTHER SEPARATIST WEAPONS DIVISIONS!!
HAVE THE GIRL BROUGHT TO ME, BIROK.
YES, SIR.

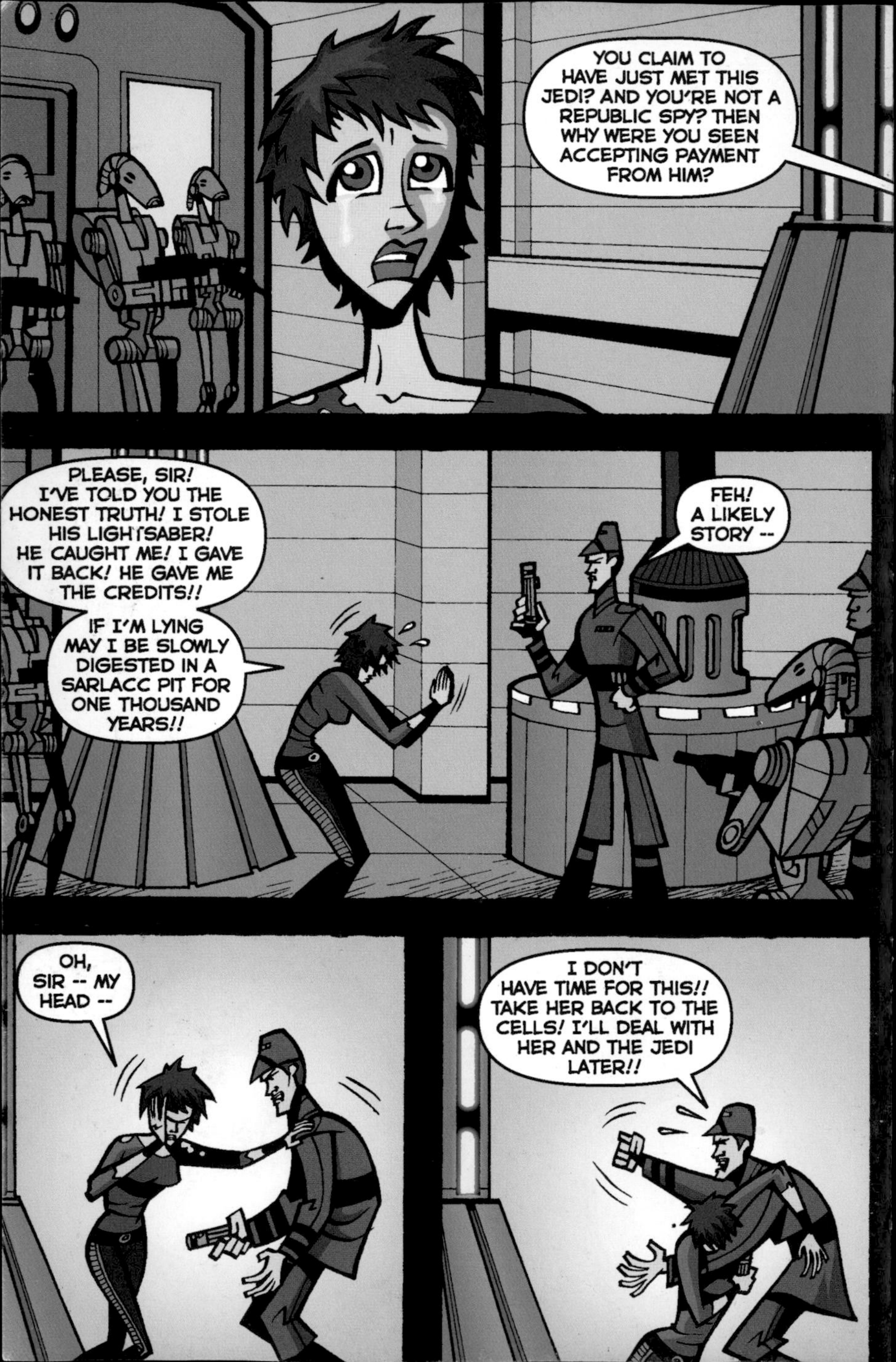
YOU CLAIM TO HAVE JUST MET THIS JEDI? AND YOU'RE NOT A REPUBLIC SPY? THEN WHY WERE YOU SEEN ACCEPTING PAYMENT FROM HIM?
PLEASE, SIR! I'VE TOLD YOU THE HONEST TRUTH! I STOLE HIS LIGHTSABER! HE CAUGHT ME! I GAVE IT BACK! HE GAVE ME THE CREDITS!!
IF I'M LYING MAY I BE SLOWLY DIGESTED IN A SARLACC PIT FOR ONE THOUSAND YEARS!!
FEH! A LIKELY STORY --
OH, SIR -- MY HEAD --
I DON'T HAVE TIME FOR THIS!! TAKE HER BACK TO THE CELLS! I'LL DEAL WITH HER AND THE JEDI LATER!!

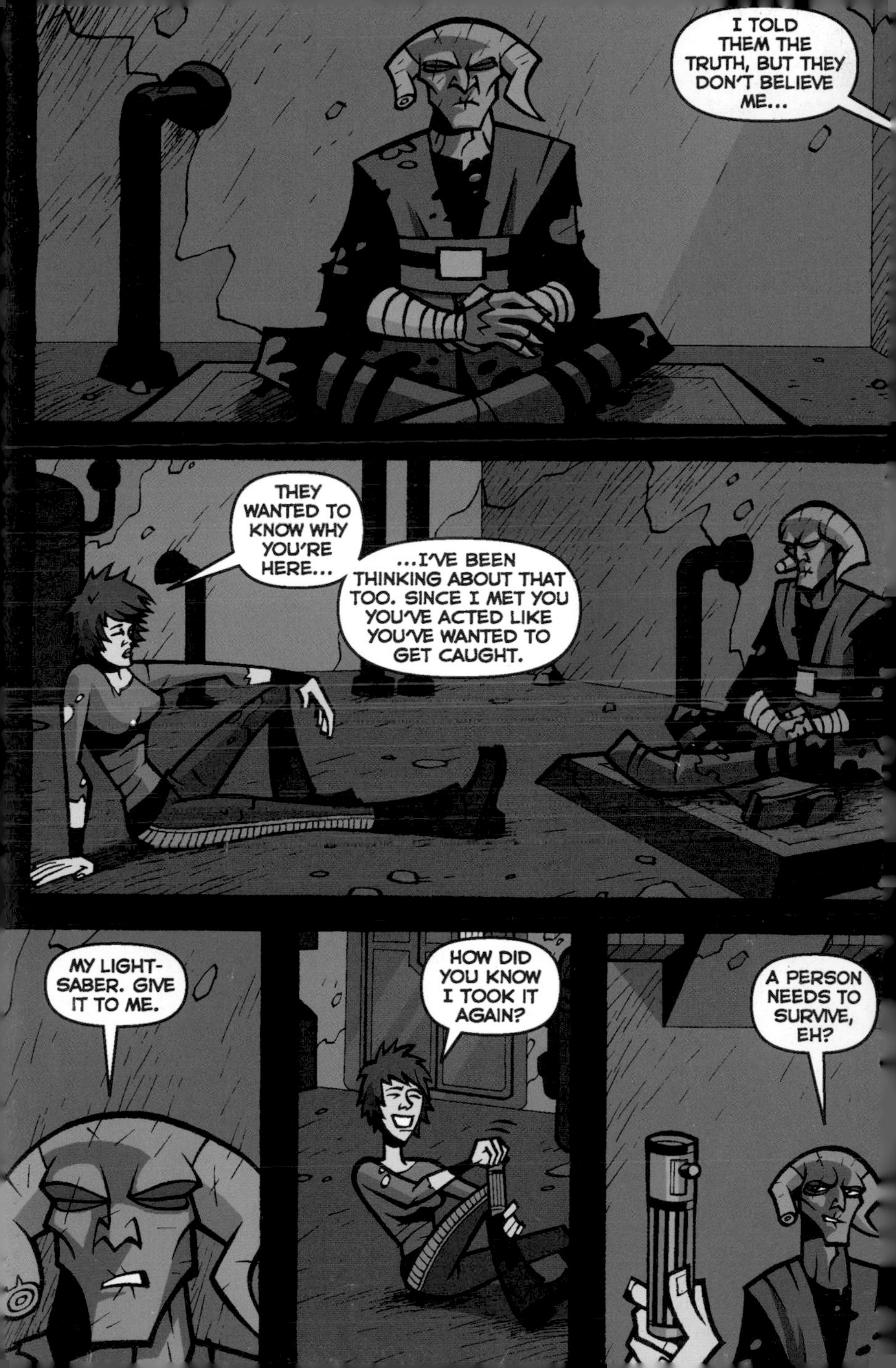
I TOLD THEM THE TRUTH, BUT THEY DON'T BELIEVE ME...
THEY WANTED TO KNOW WHY YOU'RE HERE...
...I'VE BEEN THINKING ABOUT THAT TOO. SINCE I MET YOU YOU'VE ACTED LIKE YOU'VE WANTED TO GET CAUGHT.
MY LIGHT-SABER. GIVE IT TO ME.
HOW DID YOU KNOW I TOOK IT AGAIN?
A PERSON NEEDS TO SURVIVE, EH?

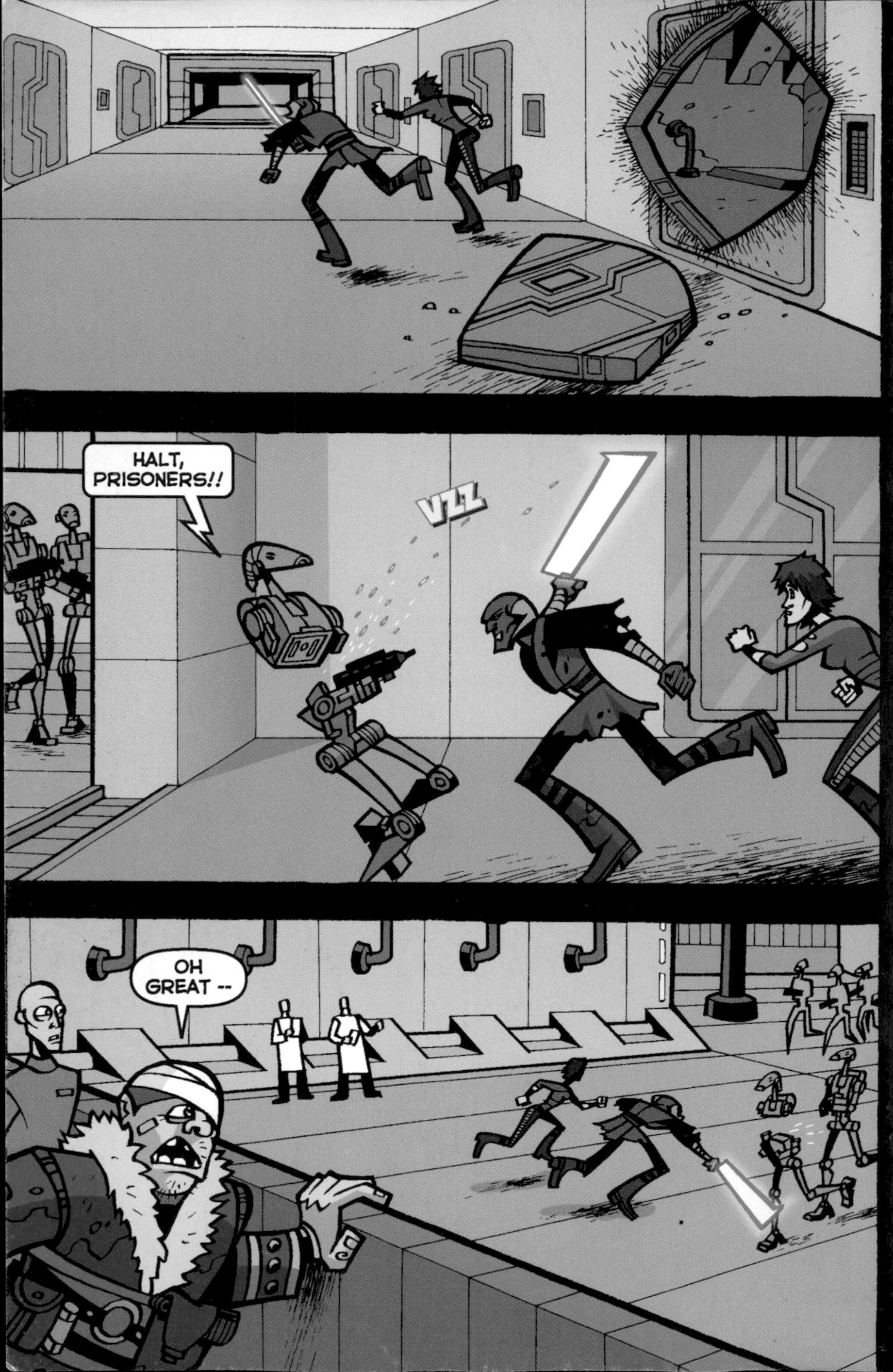
HALT, PRISONERS!!
VZZ
OH GREAT --

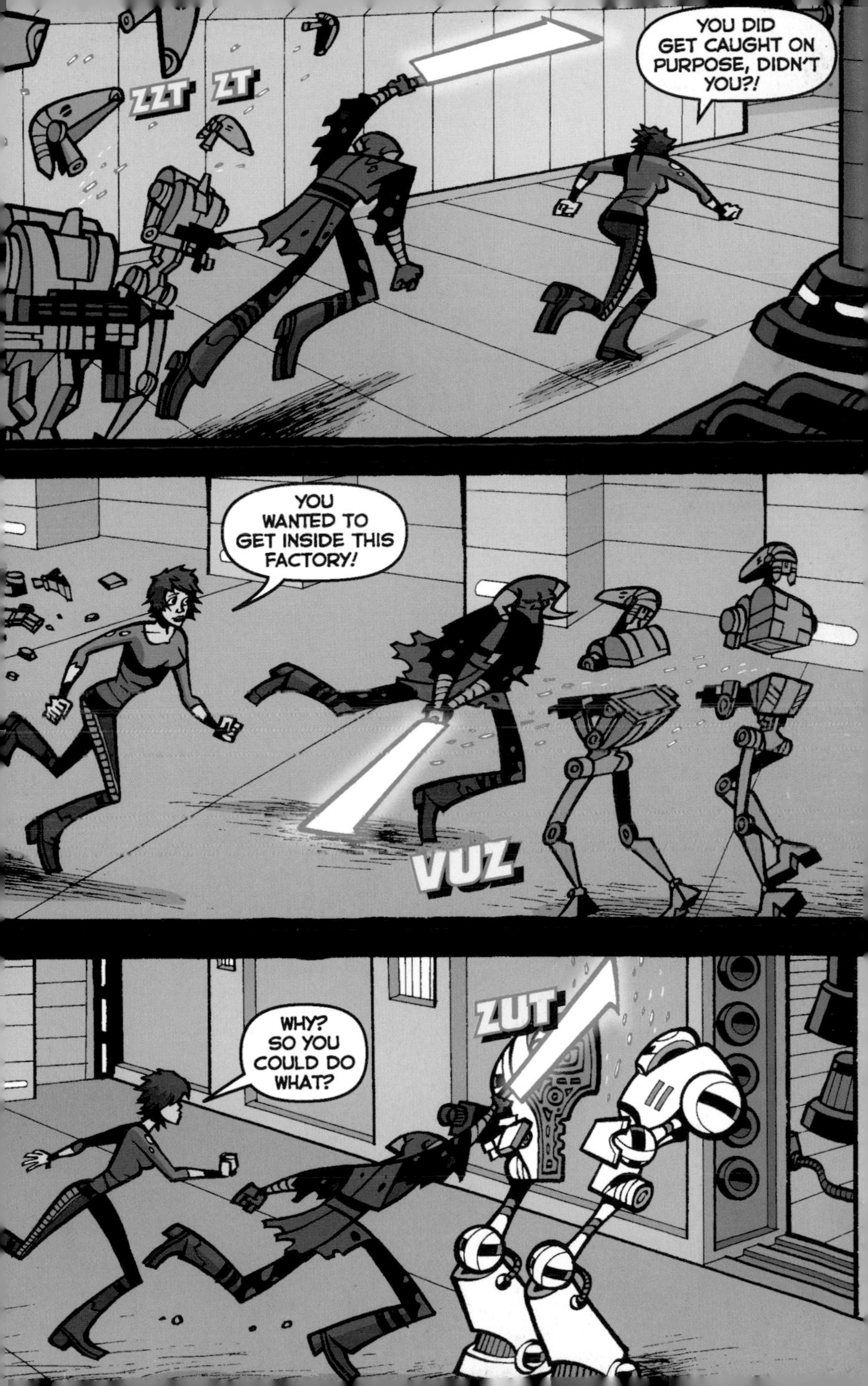
ZZT ZT
YOU DID GET CAUGHT ON PURPOSE, DIDN'T YOU?!
YOU WANTED TO GET INSIDE THIS FACTORY!
VUZ
WHY? SO YOU COULD DO WHAT?
ZUT

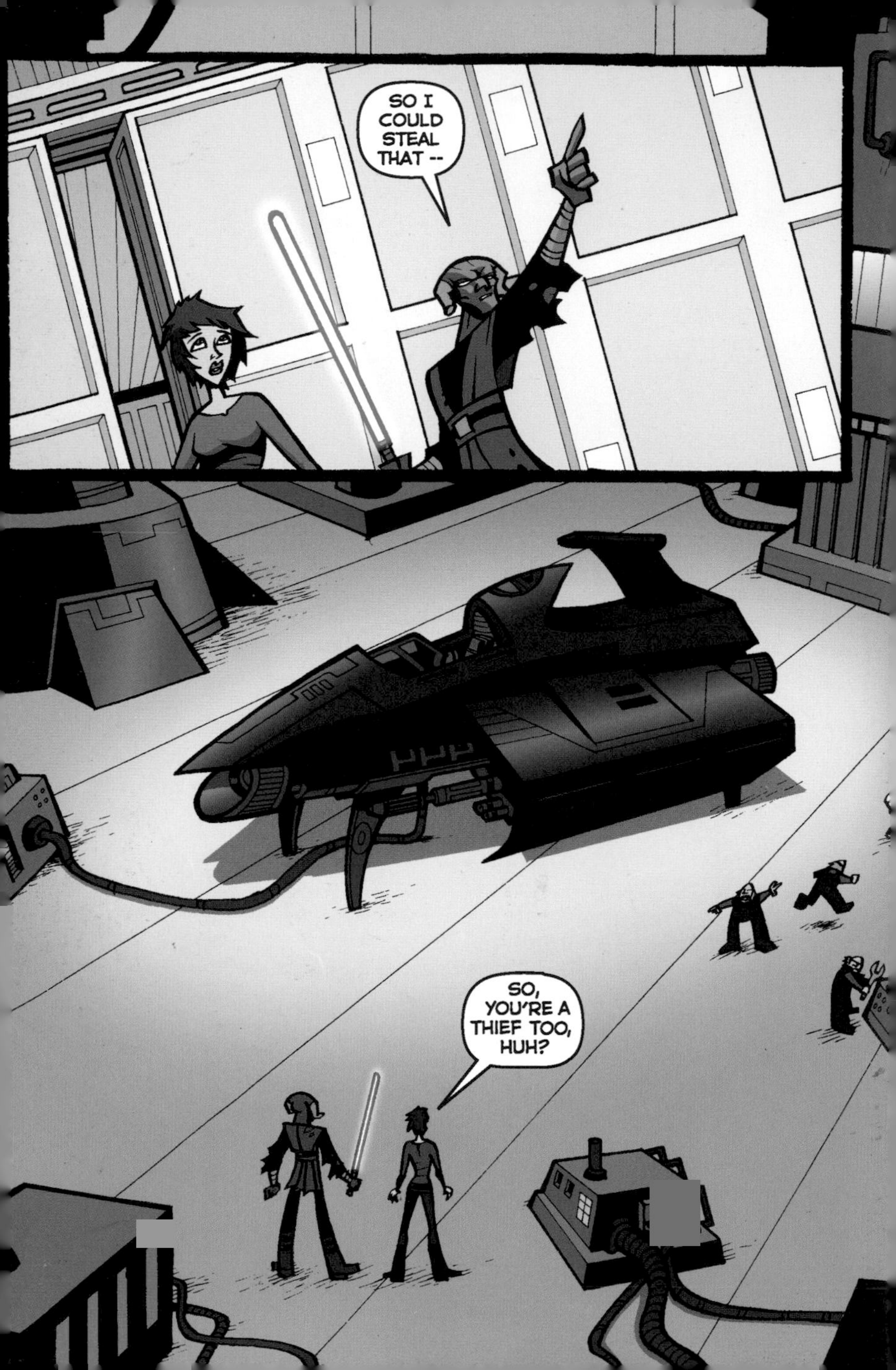
SO I COULD STEAL THAT --
SO, YOU'RE A THIEF TOO, HUH?

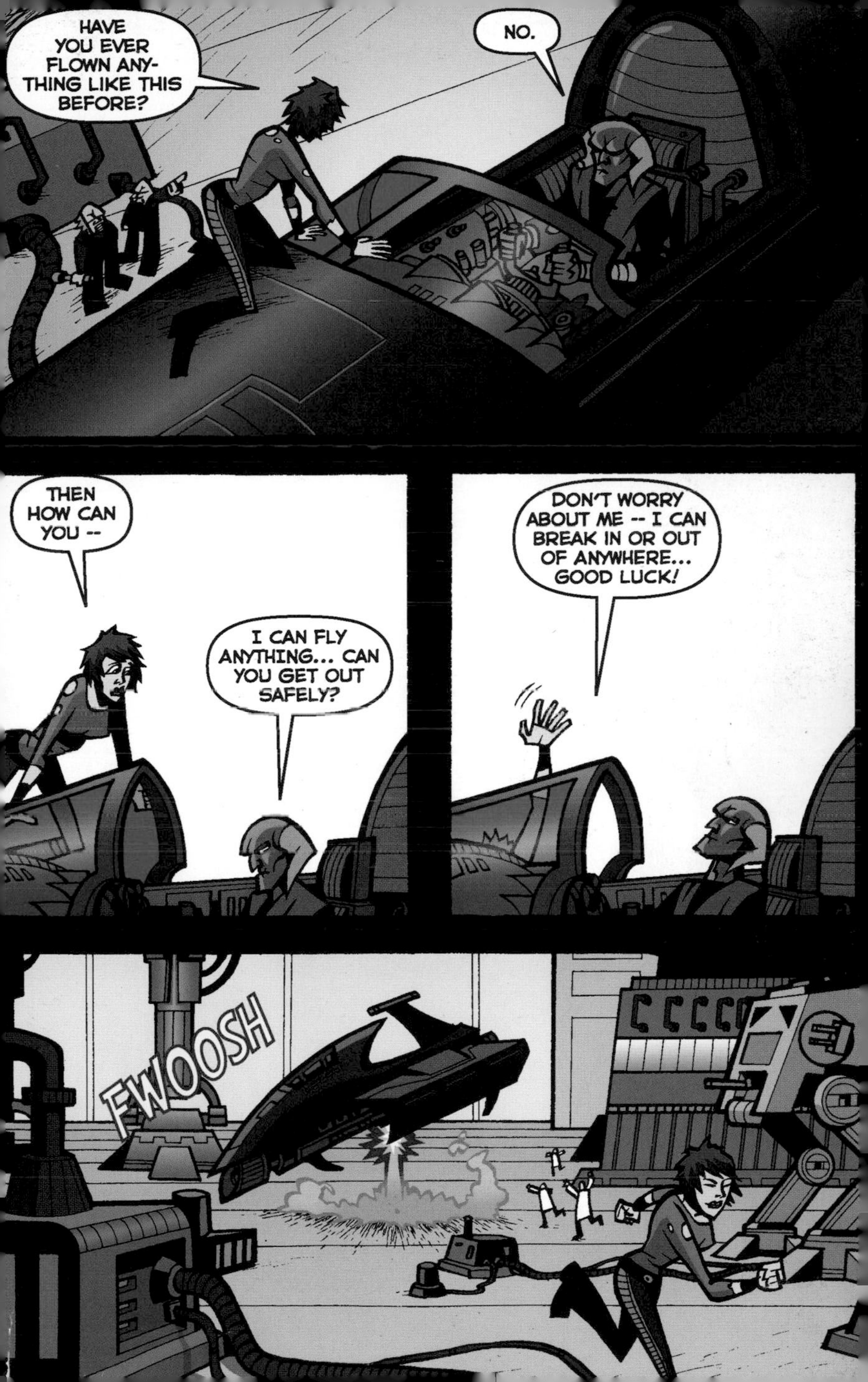

HAVE YOU EVER FLOWN ANY-THING LIKE THIS BEFORE?
NO.
THEN HOW CAN YOU --
I CAN FLY ANYTHING... CAN YOU GET OUT SAFELY?
DON'T WORRY ABOUT ME -- I CAN BREAK IN OR OUT OF ANYWHERE... GOOD LUCK!
FWOOSH

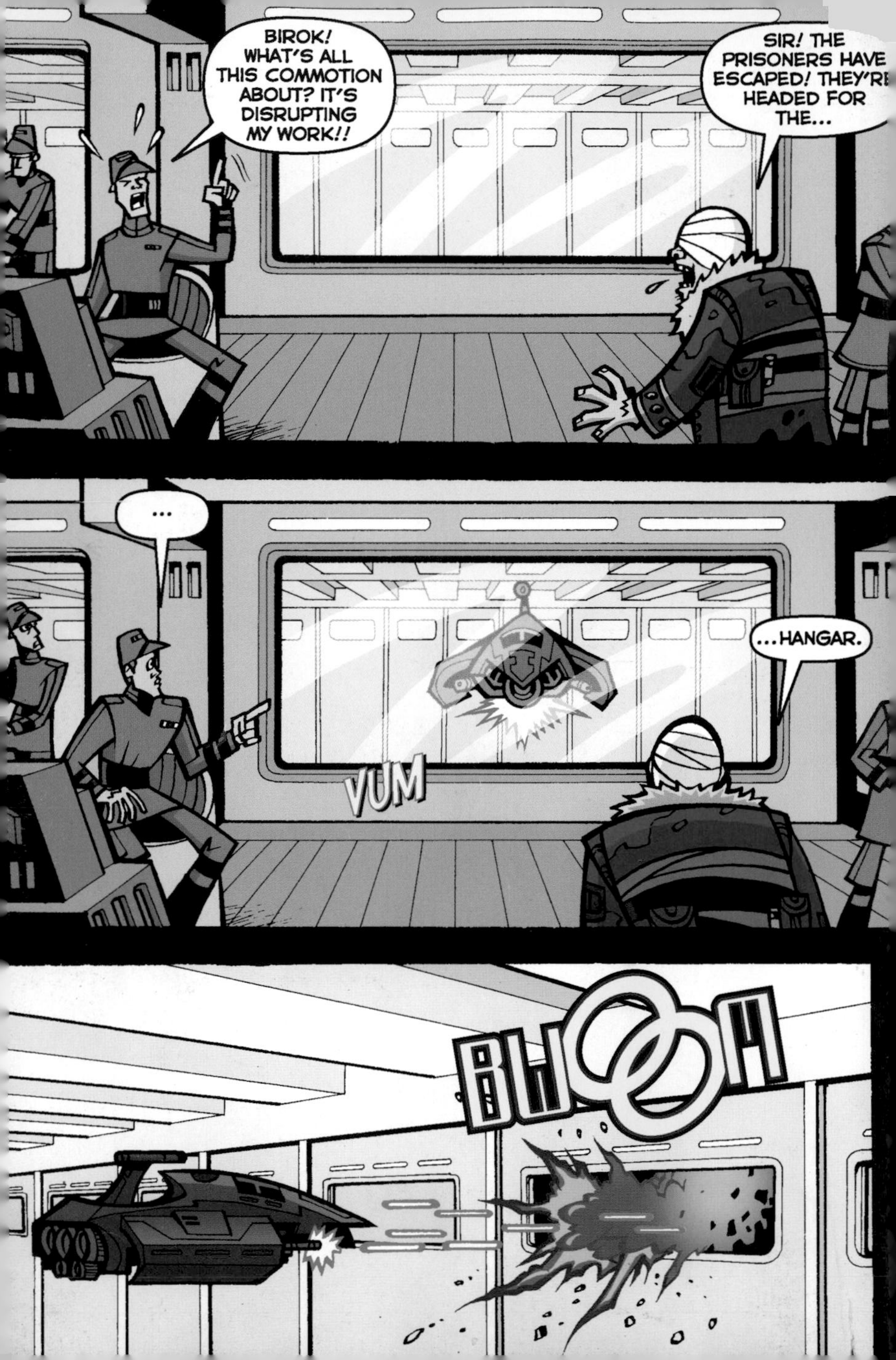
BIROK! WHAT'S ALL THIS COMMOTION ABOUT? IT'S DISRUPTING MY WORK!!
SIR! THE PRISONERS HAVE ESCAPED! THEY'RE HEADED FOR THE...
...
...HANGAR.
VUM
BLOOM

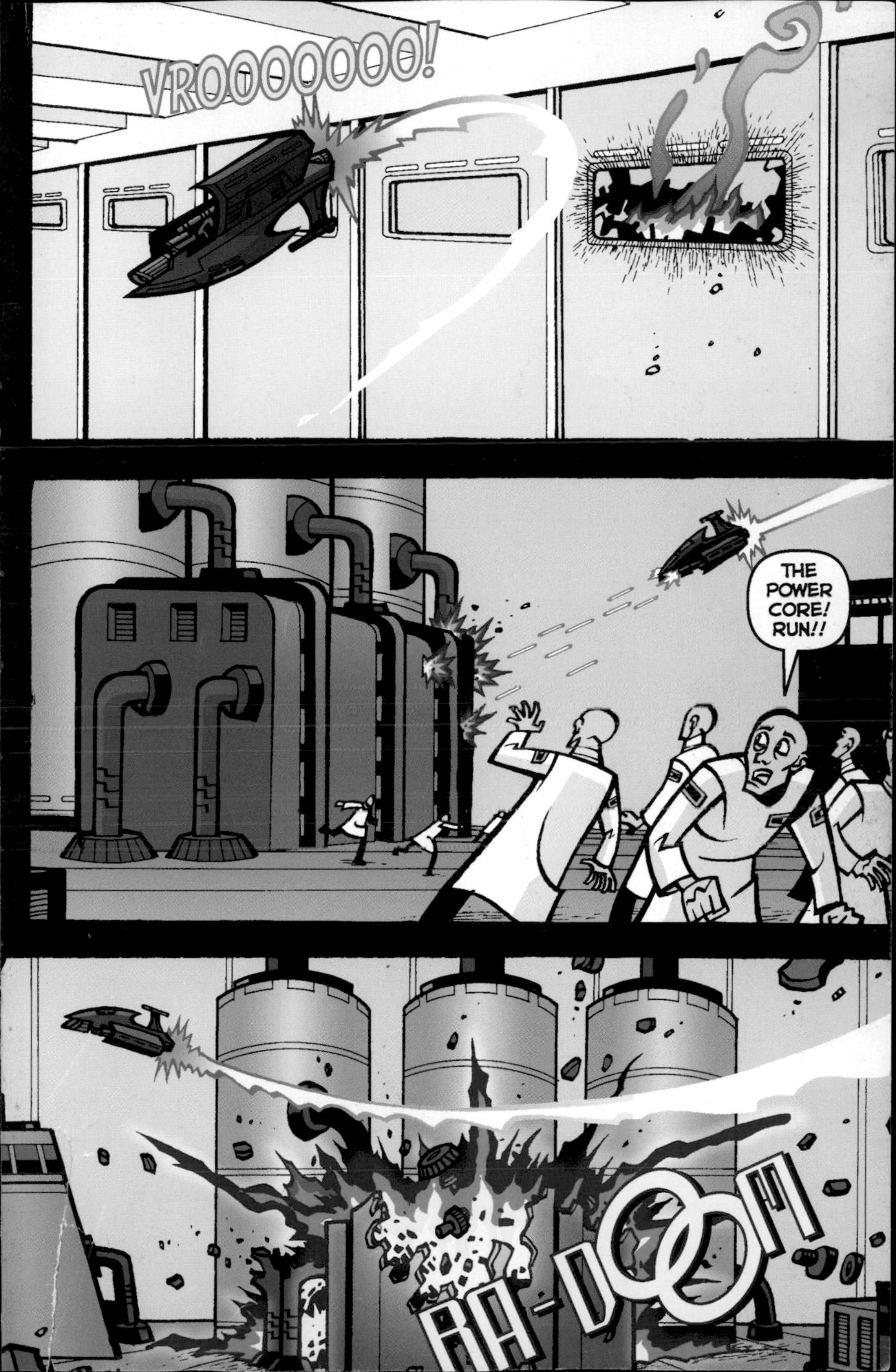
VROOOOOOO!
THE POWER CORE! RUN!!
BA-DOOM

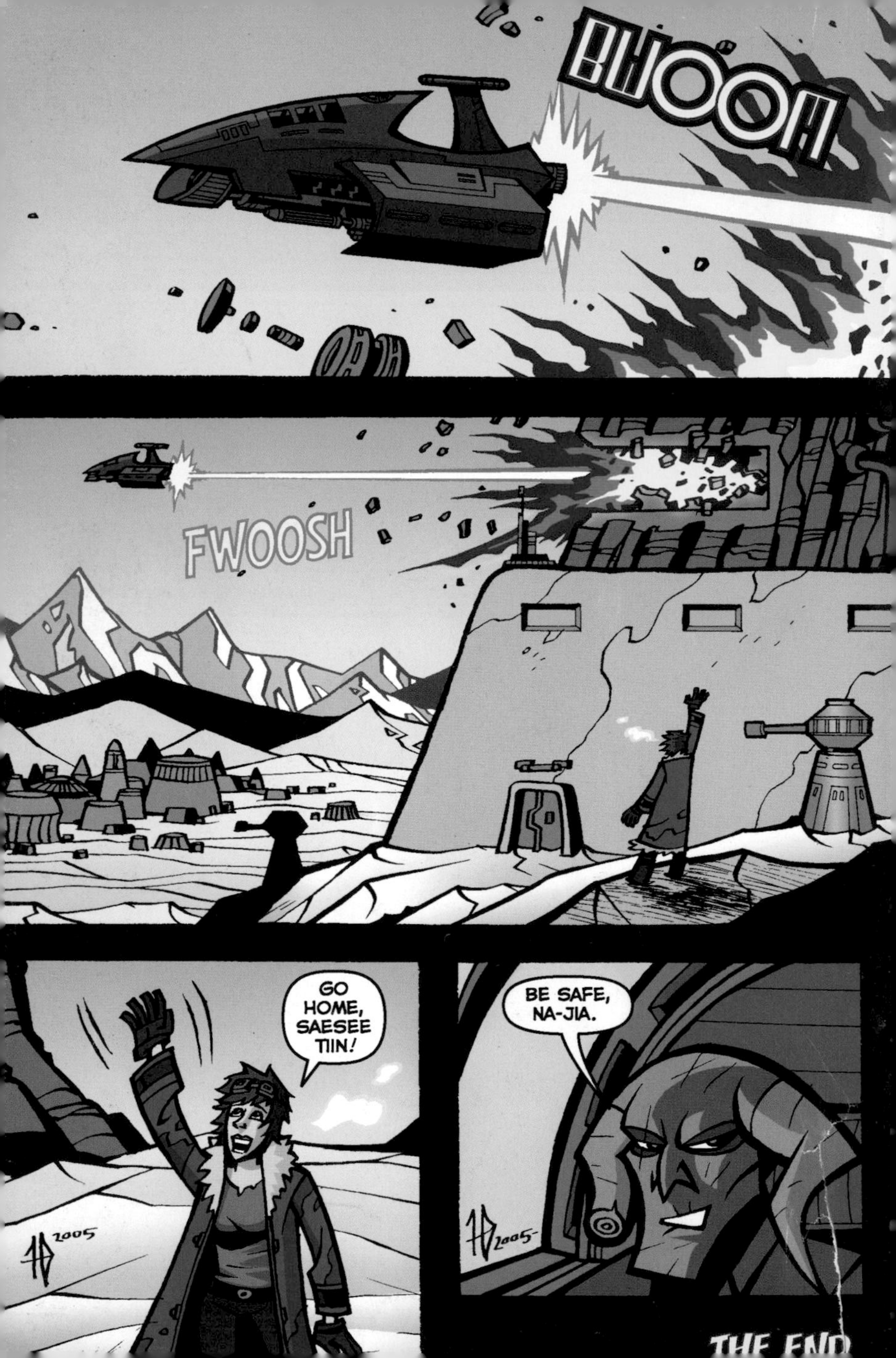
BWOOM
FWOOSH
GO HOME, SAESEE TIIN!
BE SAFE, NA-JIA.
THE END

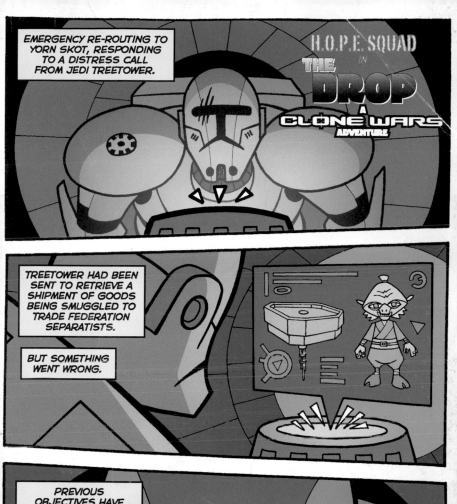

EMERGENCY RE-ROUTING TO YORN SKOT, RESPONDING TO A DISTRESS CALL FROM JEDI TREETOWER.

H.O.P.E. SQUAD IN THE DROP A CLONE WARS ADVENTURE

TREETOWER HAD BEEN SENT TO RETRIEVE A SHIPMENT OF GOODS BEING SMUGGLED TO TRADE FEDERATION SEPARATISTS.

BUT SOMETHING WENT WRONG.

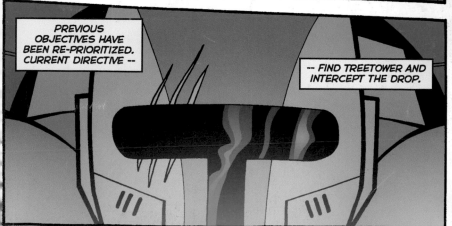

PREVIOUS OBJECTIVES HAVE BEEN RE-PRIORITIZED. CURRENT DIRECTIVE --

-- FIND TREETOWER AND INTERCEPT THE DROP.

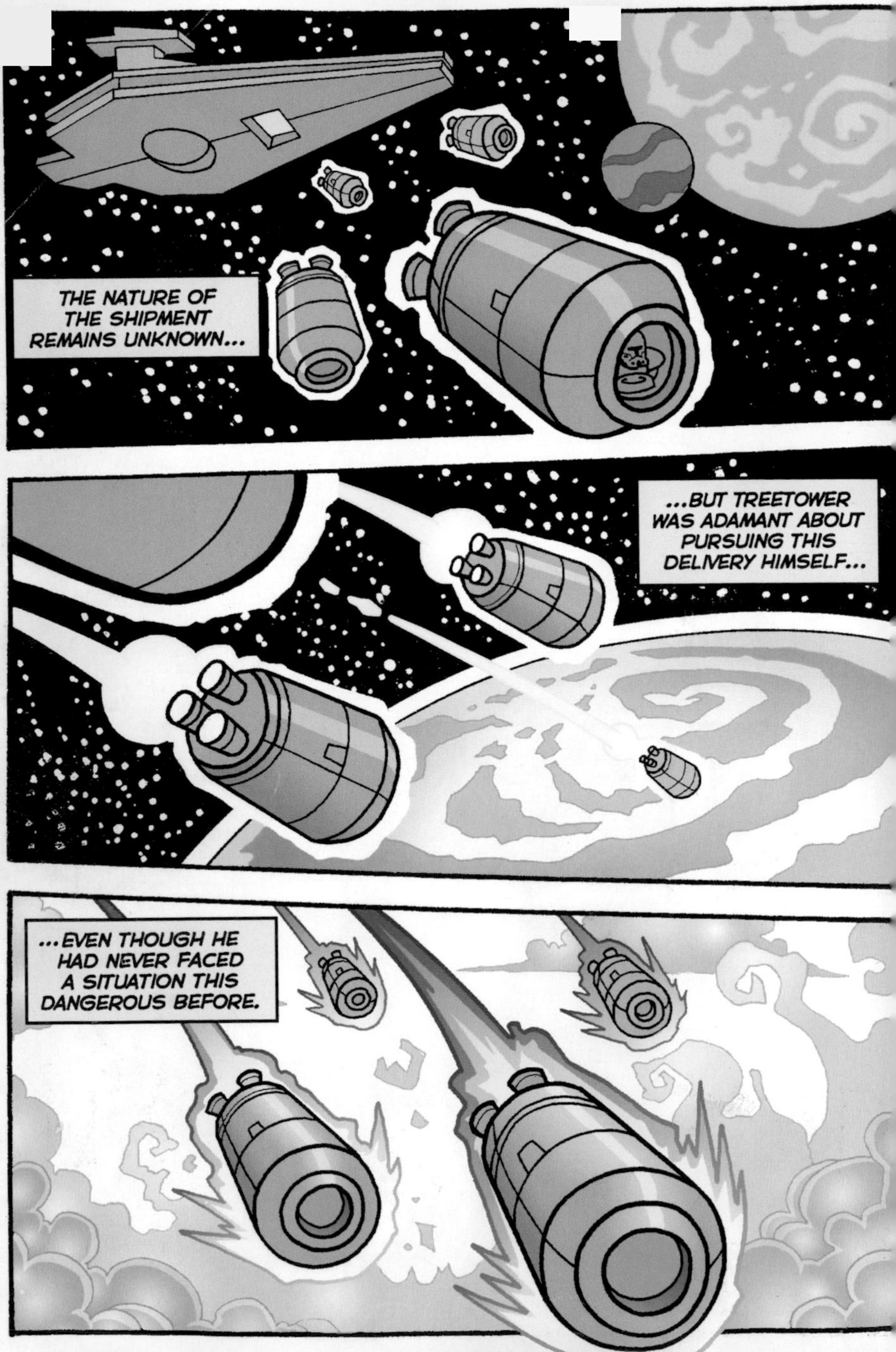
THE NATURE OF THE SHIPMENT REMAINS UNKNOWN...
...BUT TREETOWER WAS ADAMANT ABOUT PURSUING THIS DELIVERY HIMSELF...
...EVEN THOUGH HE HAD NEVER FACED A SITUATION THIS DANGEROUS BEFORE.

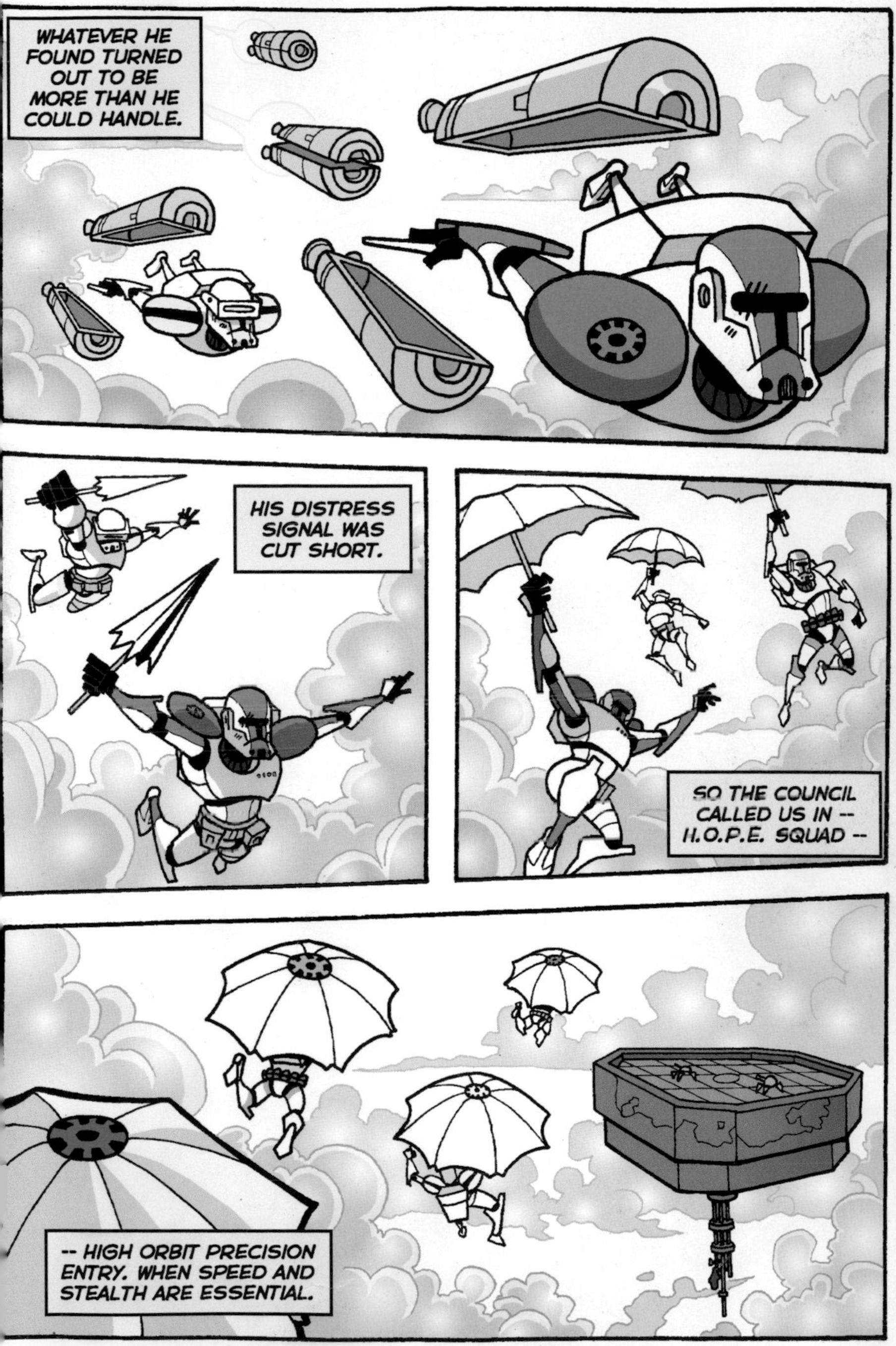
WHATEVER HE FOUND TURNED OUT TO BE MORE THAN HE COULD HANDLE.
HIS DISTRESS SIGNAL WAS CUT SHORT.
SO THE COUNCIL CALLED US IN -- H.O.P.E. SQUAD --
-- HIGH ORBIT PRECISION ENTRY. WHEN SPEED AND STEALTH ARE ESSENTIAL.

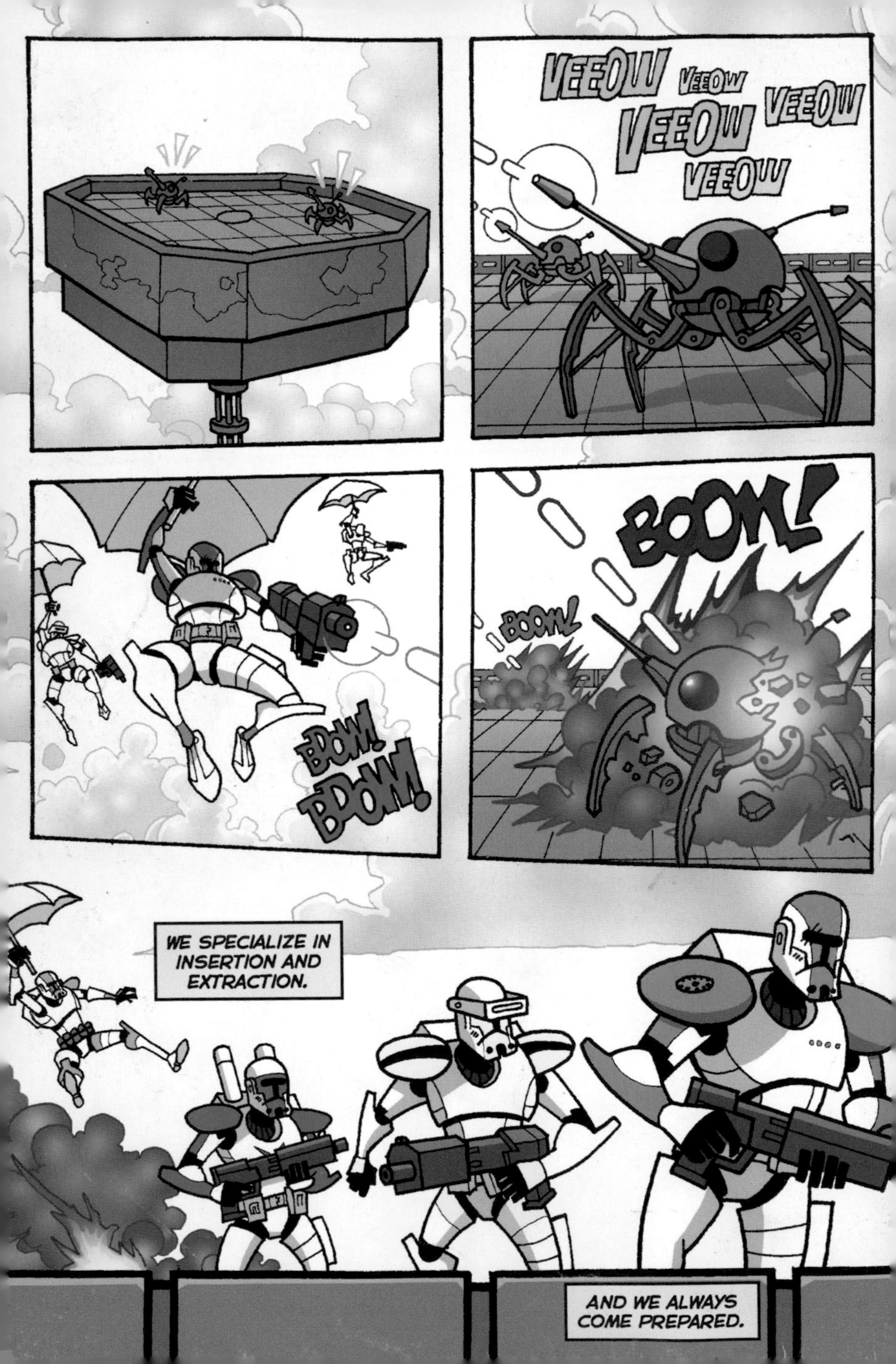

VEEOW VEEOW VEEOW VEEOW VEEOW
BOOM! BOOM!
BOOM!
BOOM!
WE SPECIALIZE IN INSERTION AND EXTRACTION.
AND WE ALWAYS COME PREPARED.

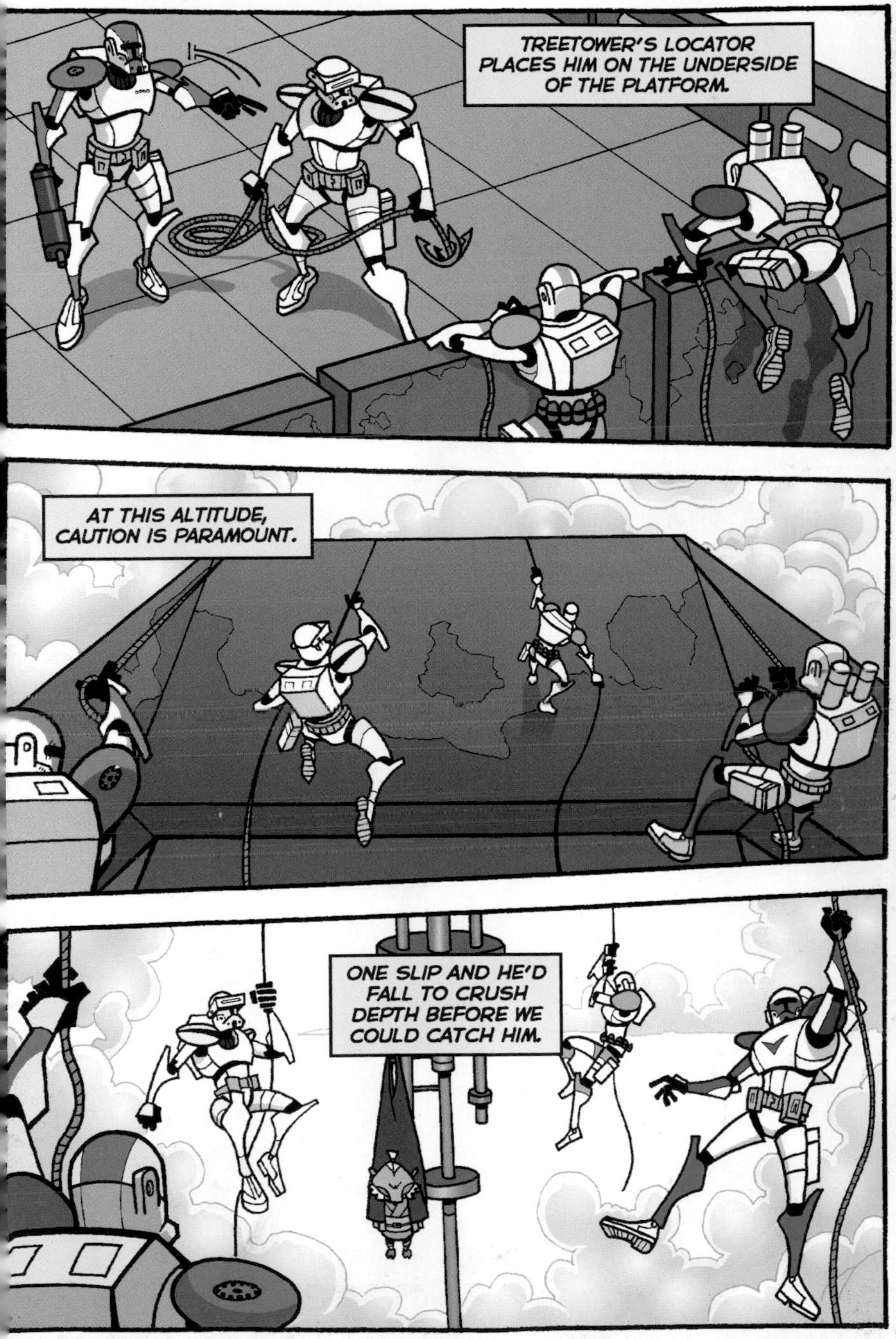
TREETOWER'S LOCATOR PLACES HIM ON THE UNDERSIDE OF THE PLATFORM.
AT THIS ALTITUDE, CAUTION IS PARAMOUNT.
ONE SLIP AND HE'D FALL TO CRUSH DEPTH BEFORE WE COULD CATCH HIM.

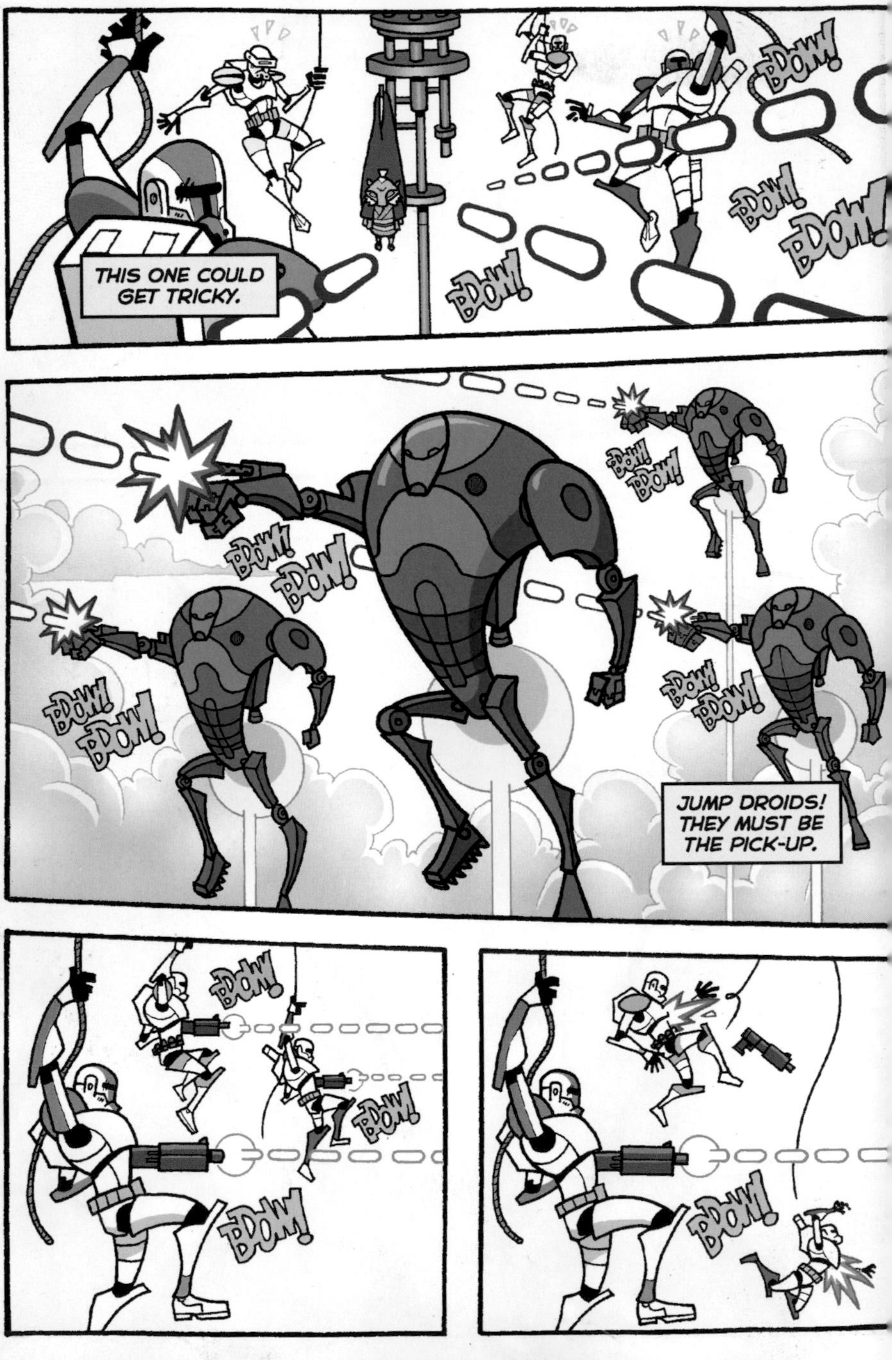
BDOW!
BDOW!
BDOW!
THIS ONE COULD GET TRICKY.
BDOW!
BDOW!
BDOW!
BDOW!
BDOW!
BDOW!
BDOW!
BDOW!
BDOW!
JUMP DROIDS! THEY MUST BE THE PICK-UP.
BDOW!
BDOW!
BDOW!
BDOW!

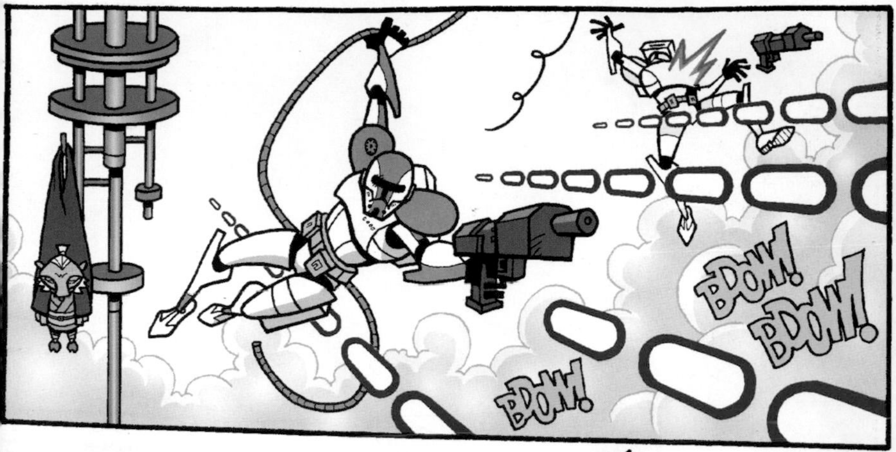
BDOW!
BDOW!
BDOW!

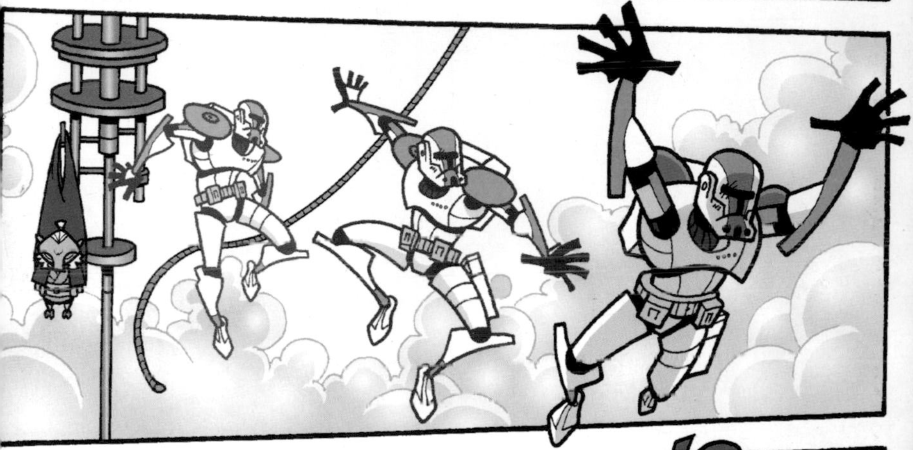

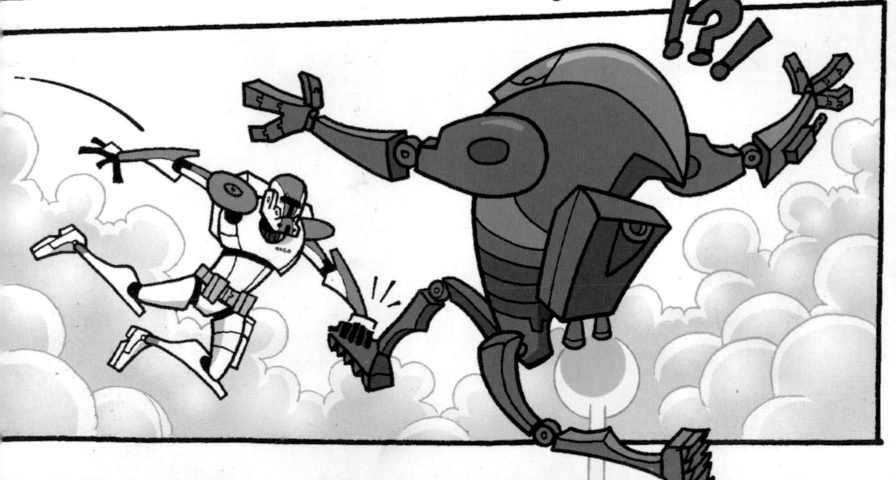
!?!

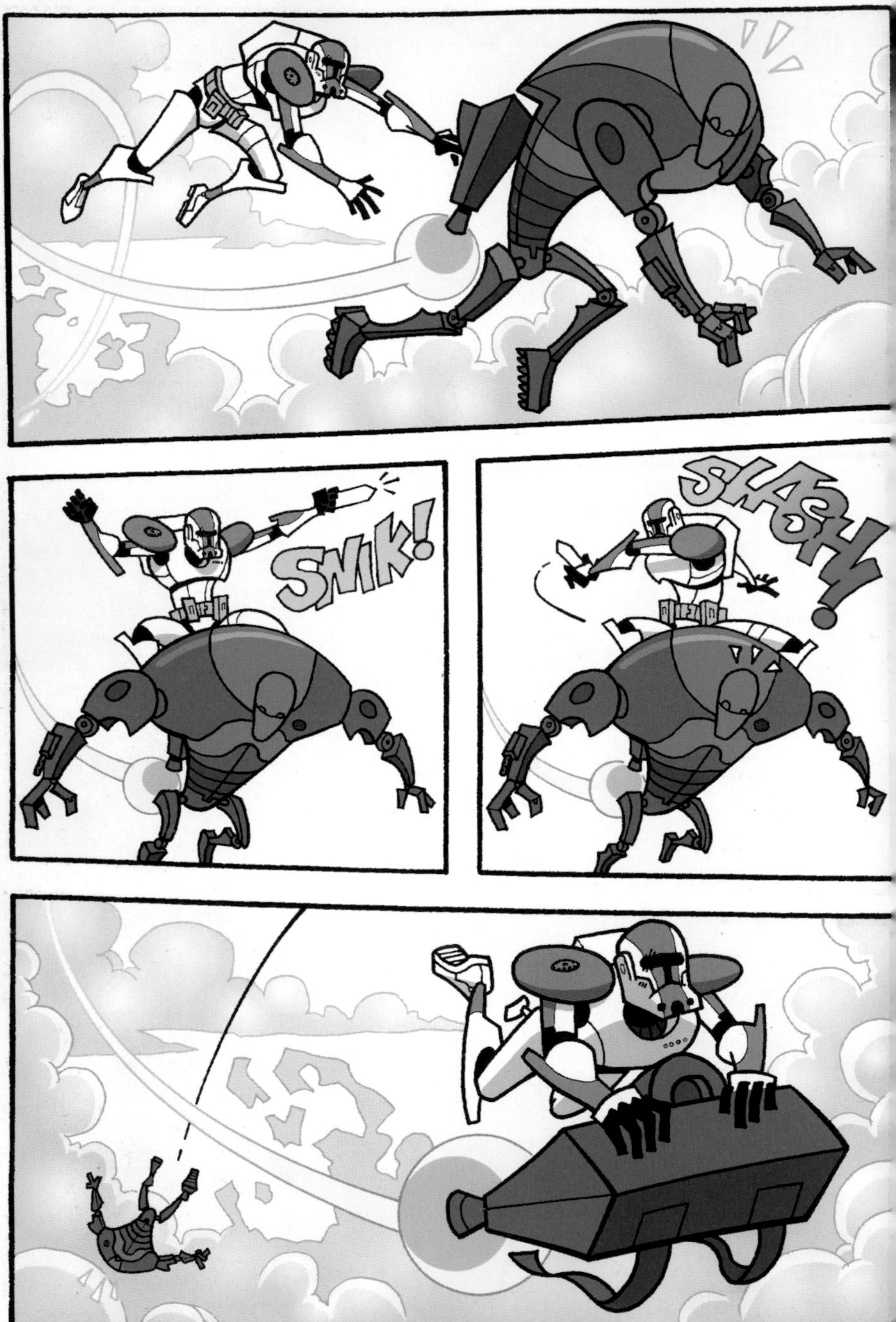
SNIK!
SLASH!

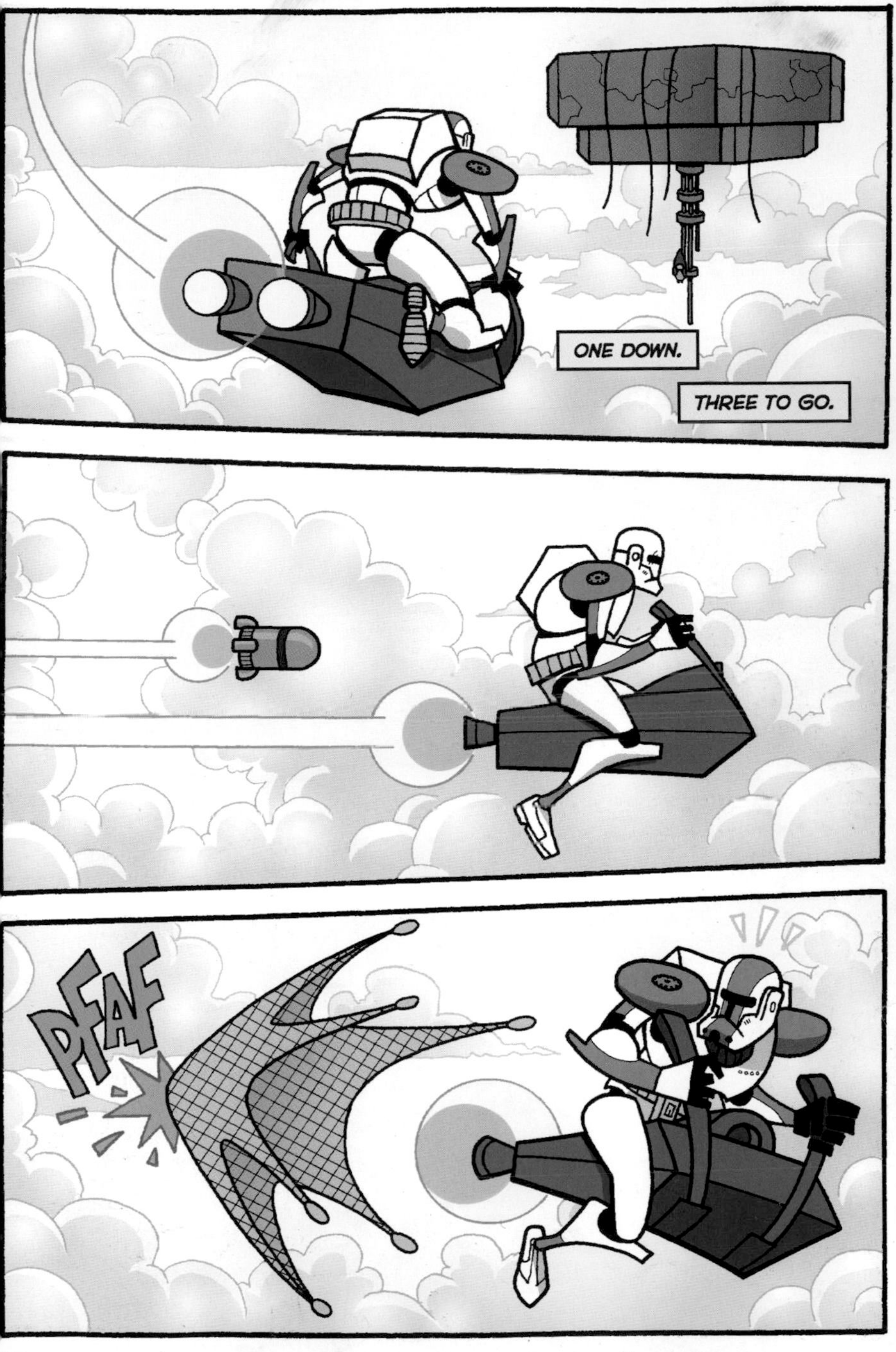
ONE DOWN.
THREE TO GO.
PFAF

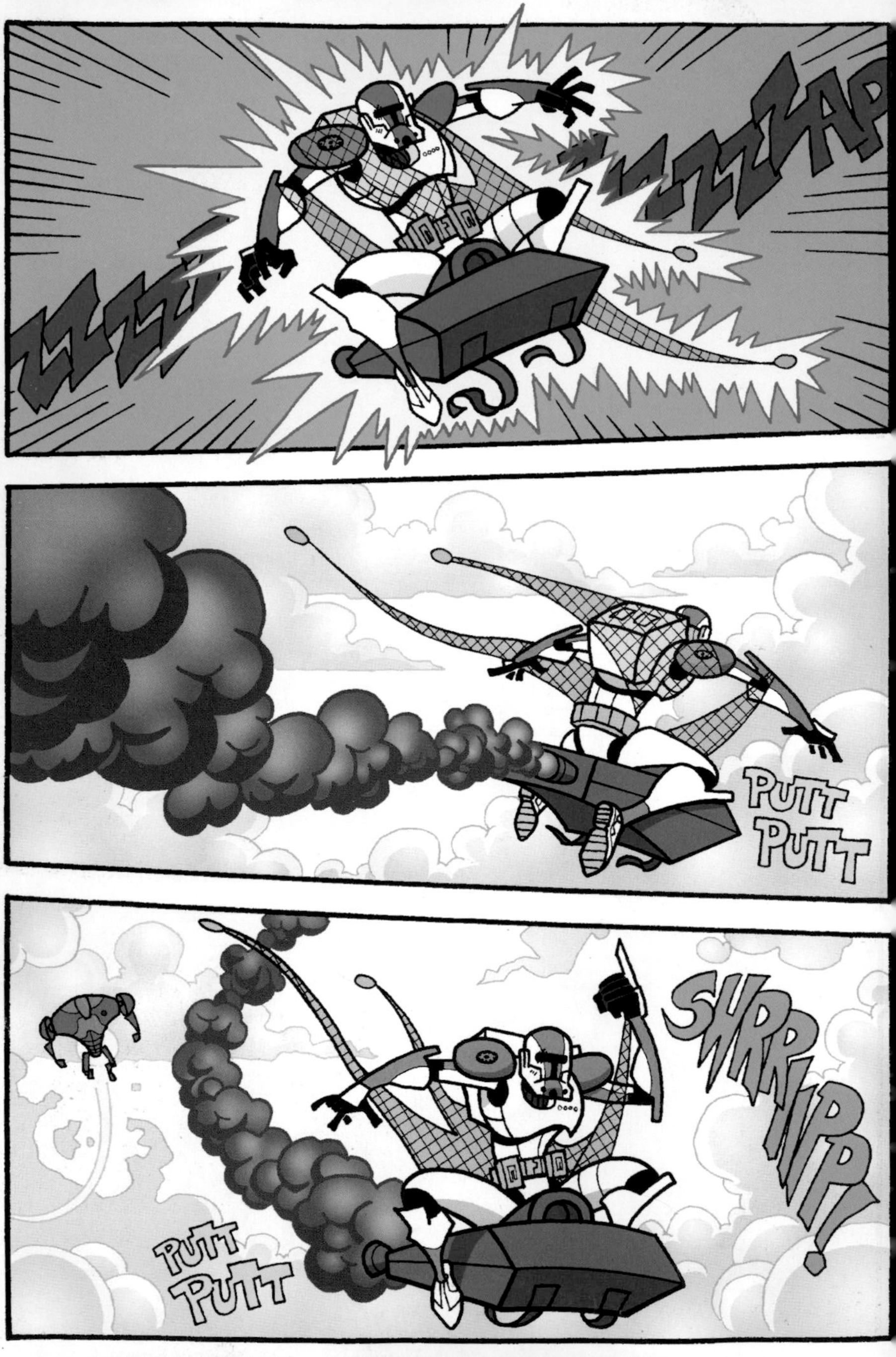
ZZZZ
ZZZZAP
PUTT PUTT
SHRRIPP!
PUTT PUTT

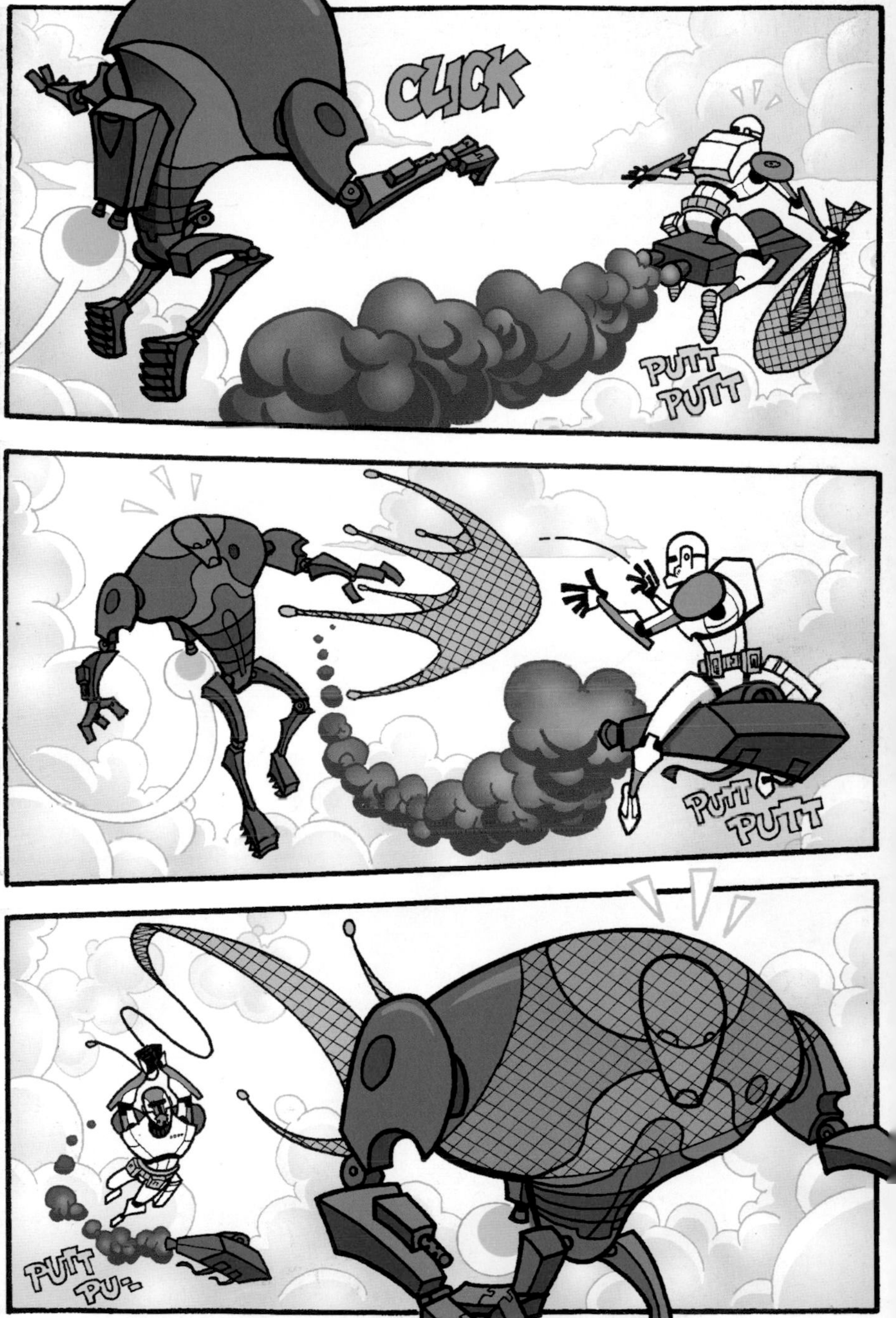
CLICK
PUTT
PUTT
PUTT
PUTT
PUTT
PU-

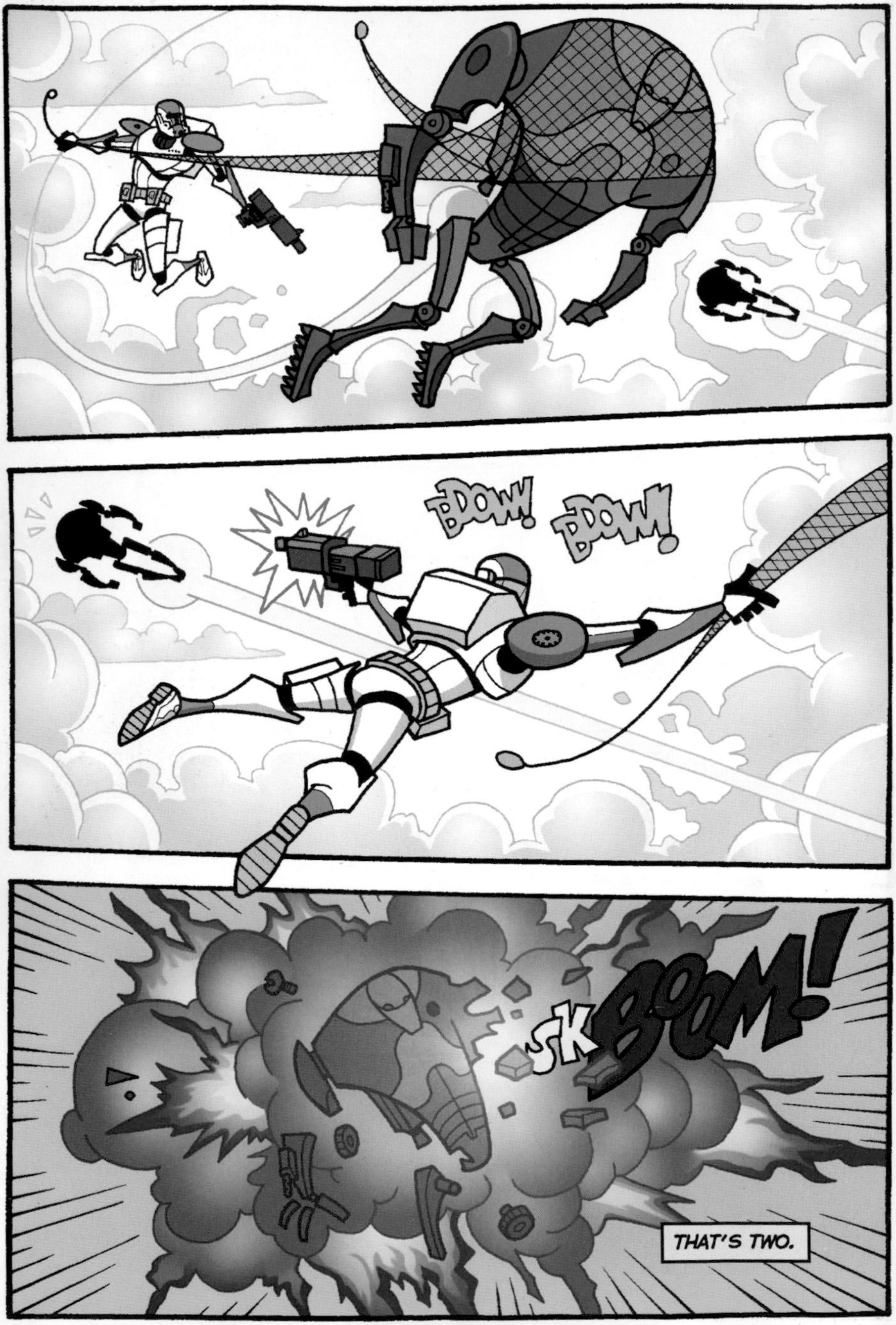
BDOWM!
BDOWM!
SKBOOM!
THAT'S TWO.

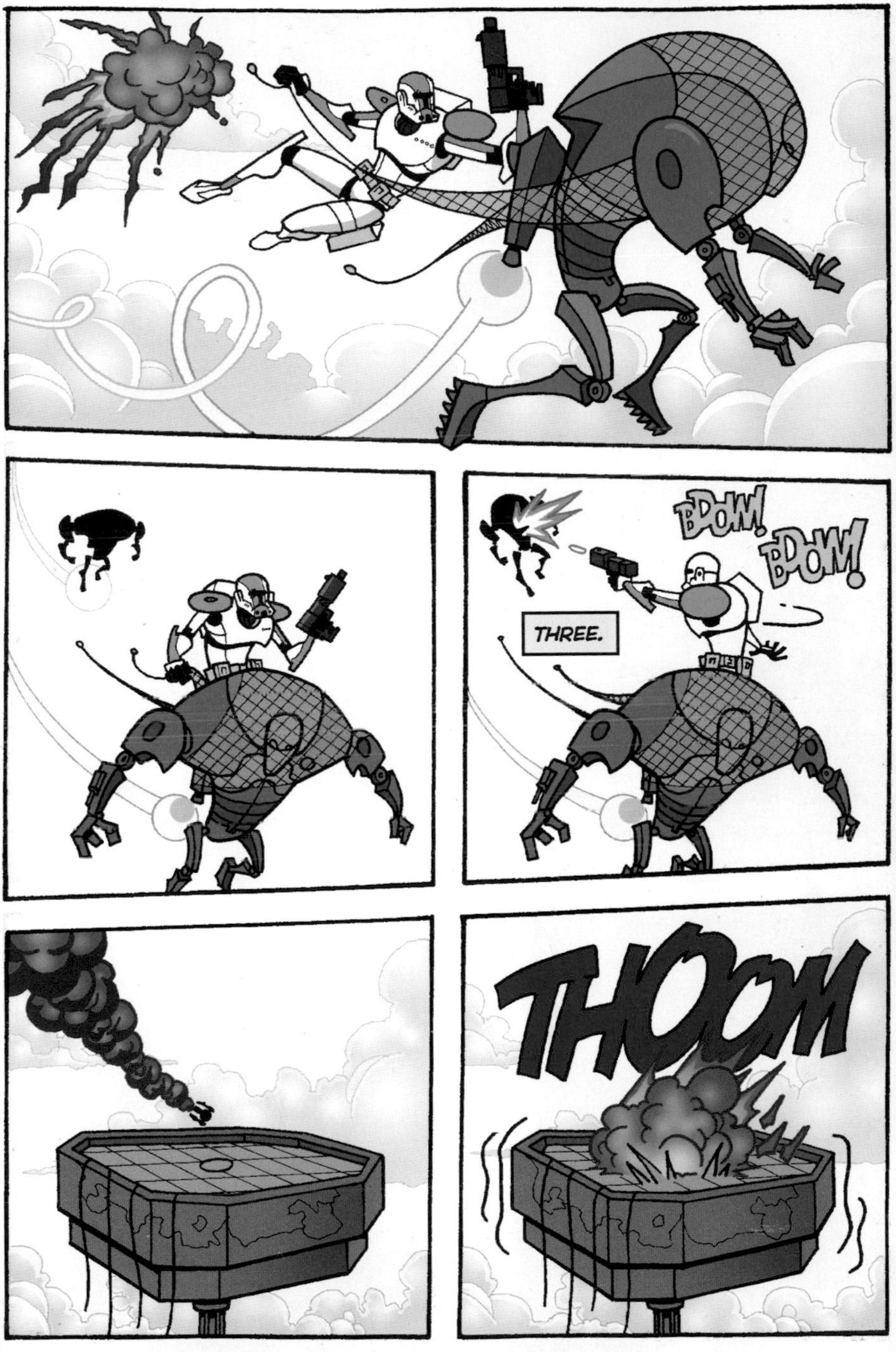
BDOW! BDOW!
THREE.
THOOM

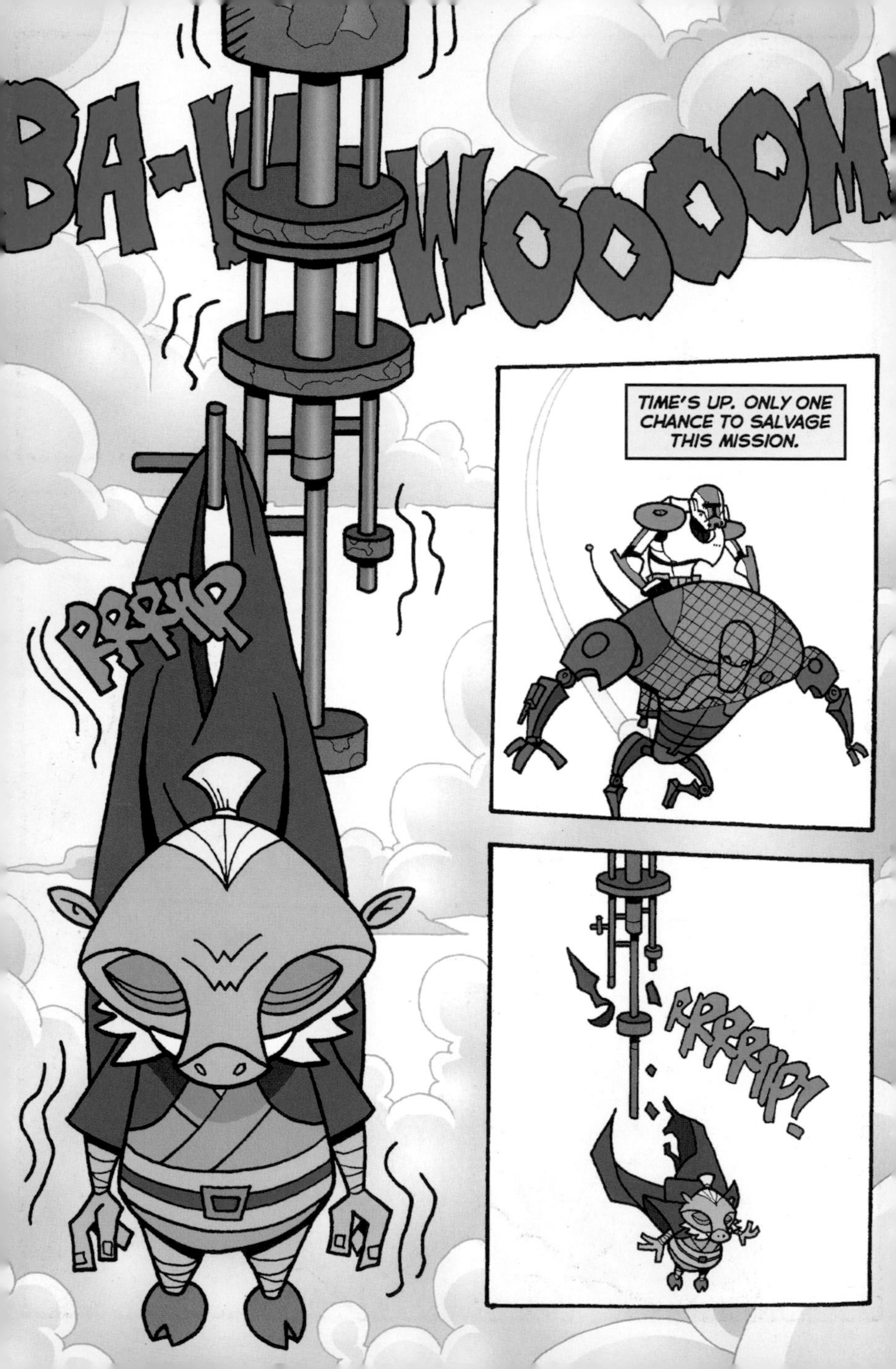
BA-WHOOOOM!
RRRIP
TIME'S UP. ONLY ONE CHANCE TO SALVAGE THIS MISSION.
RRRRIIP!

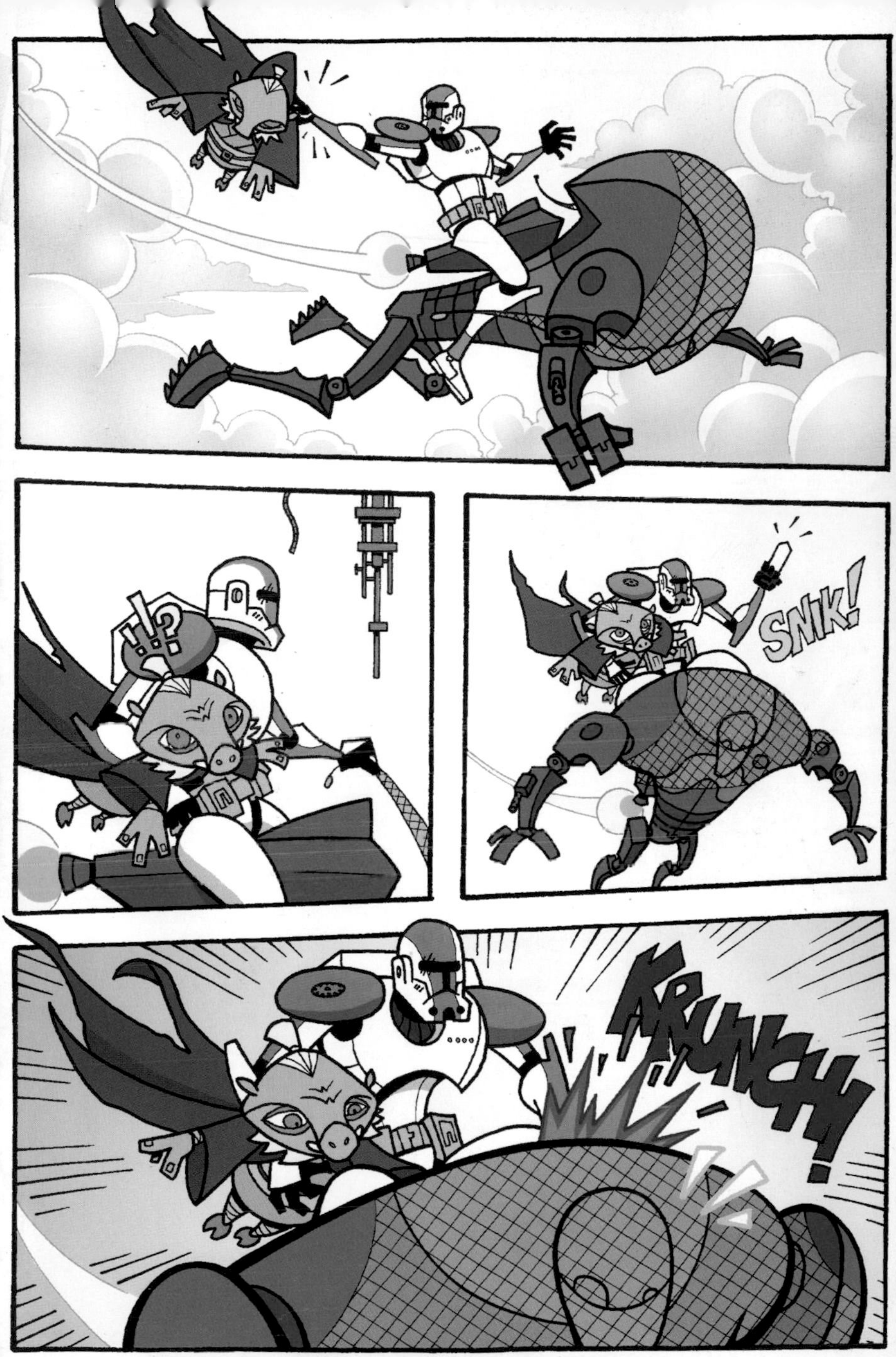
!?
SNIK!
KRUNCH!

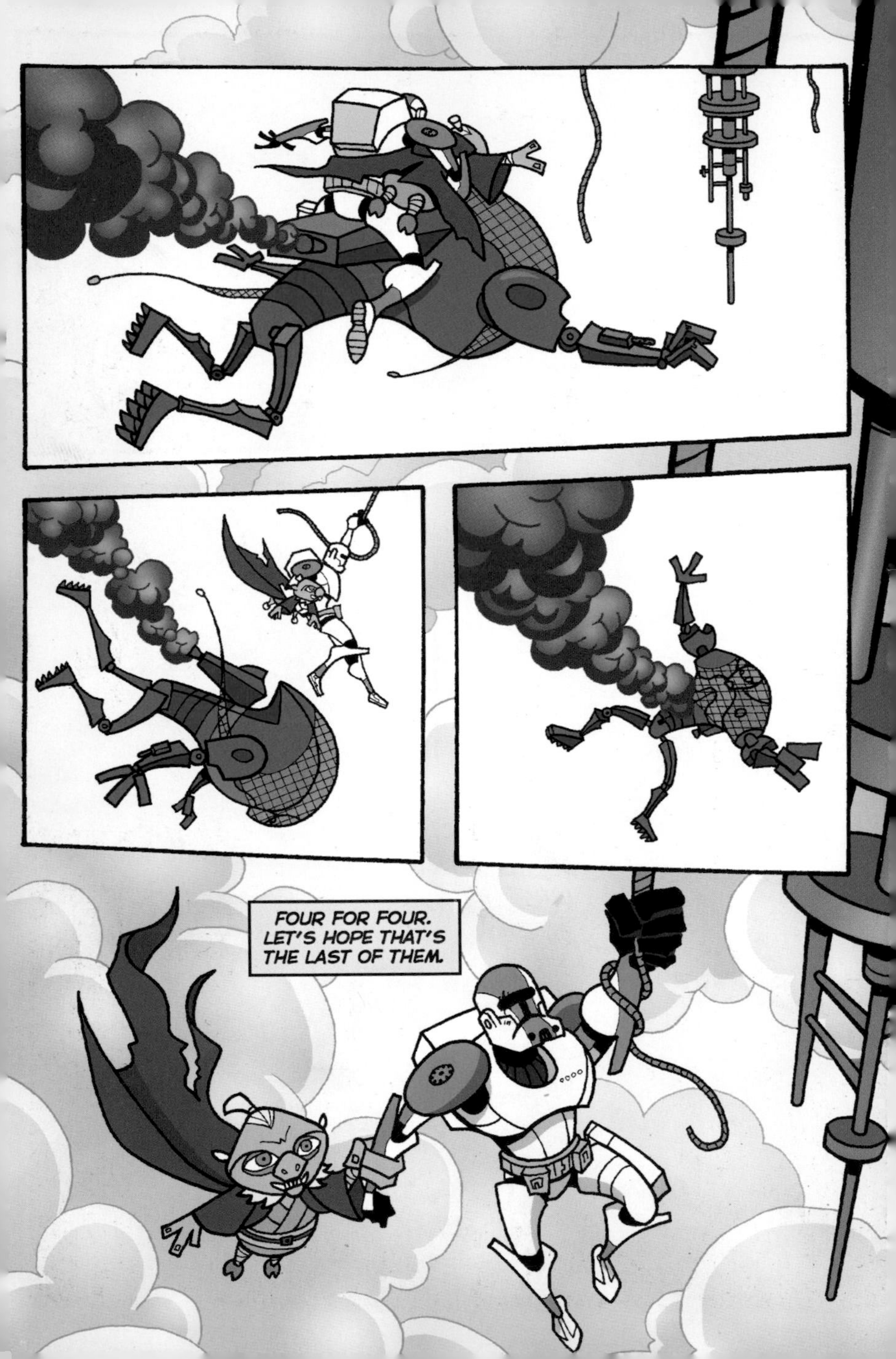
FOUR FOR FOUR. LET'S HOPE THAT'S THE LAST OF THEM.

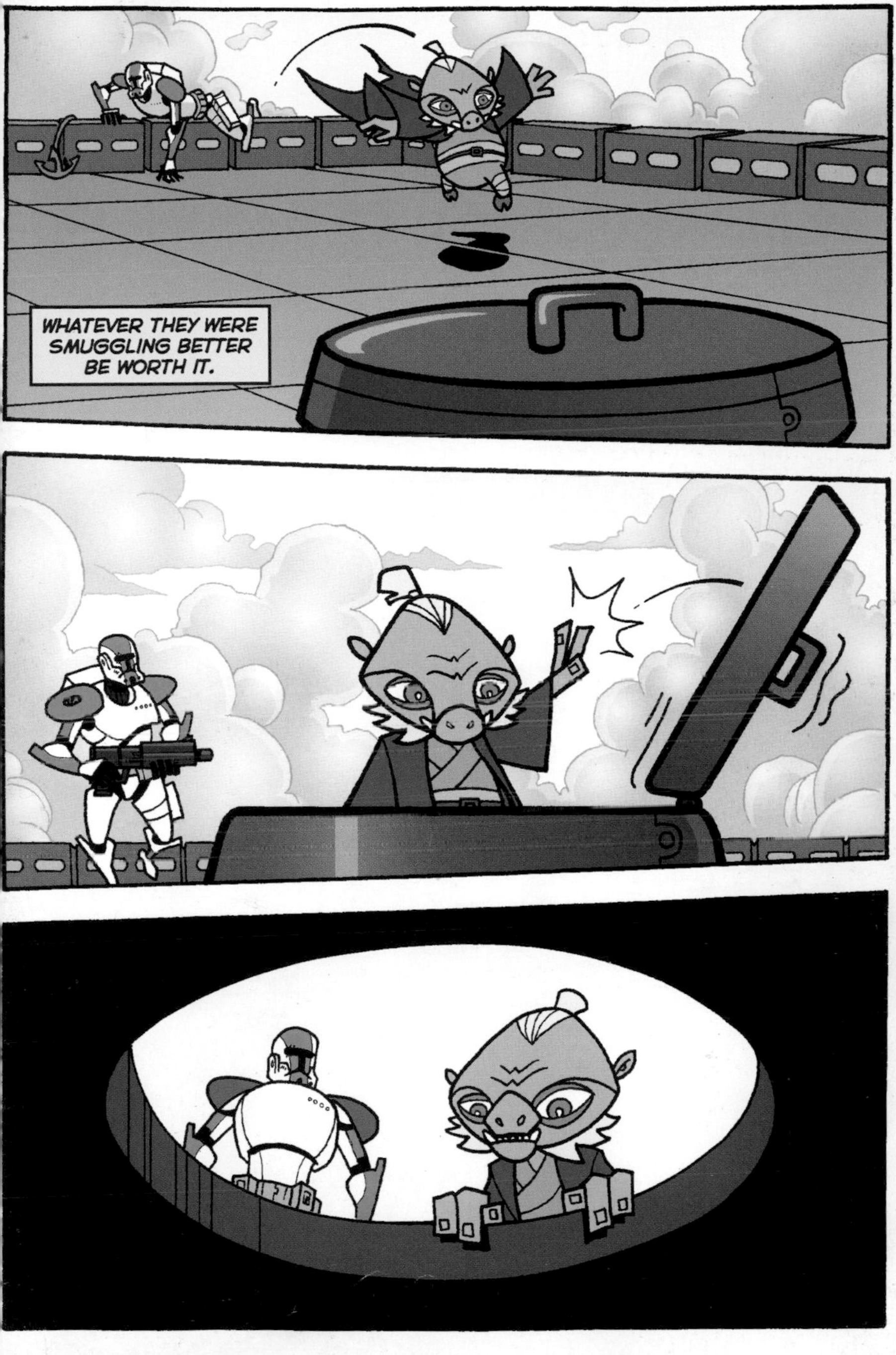
WHATEVER THEY WERE SMUGGLING BETTER BE WORTH IT.

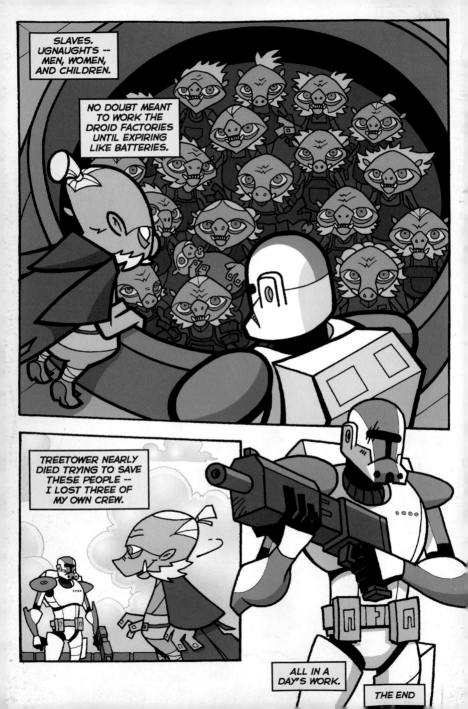

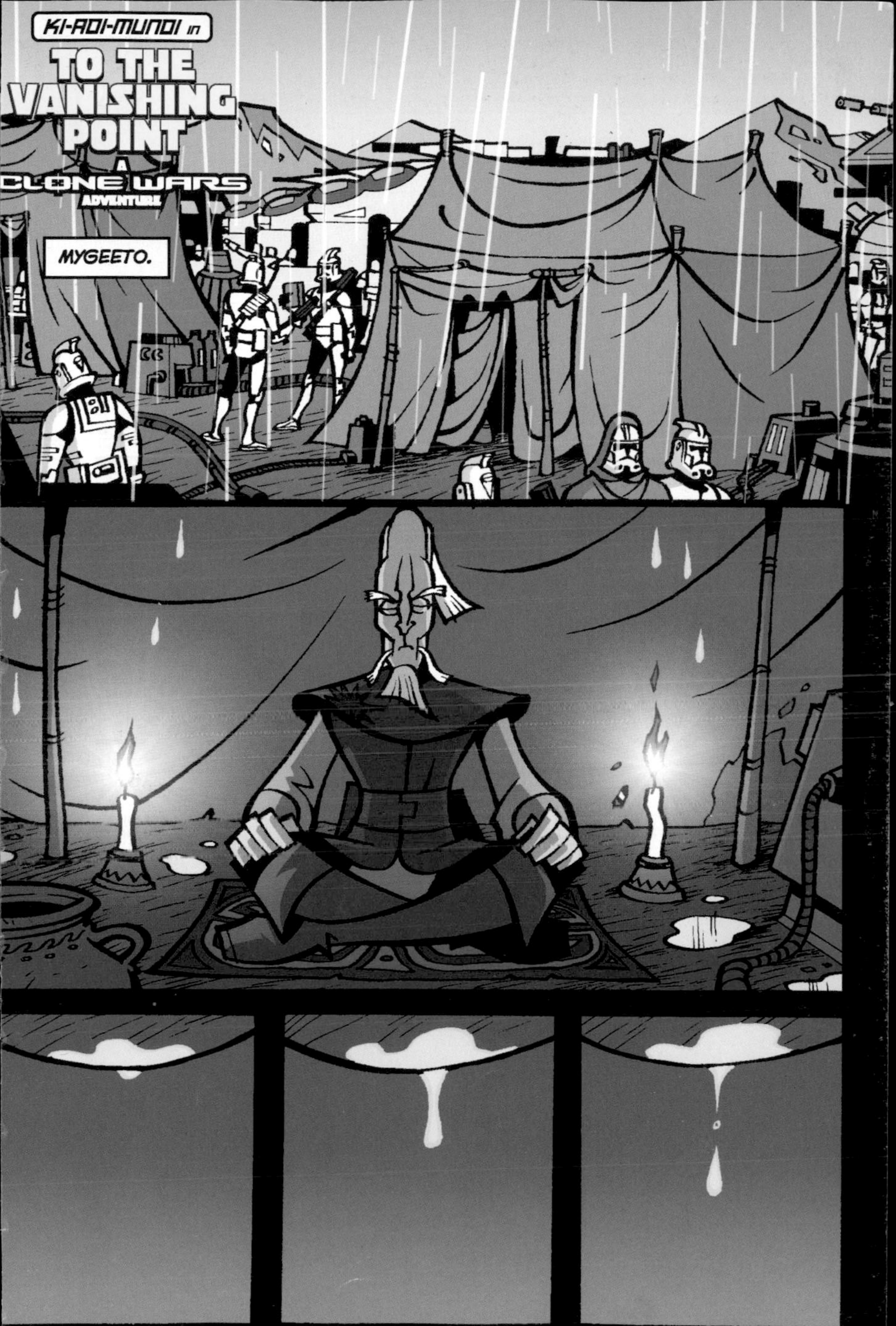
KI-ADI-MUNDI in
TO THE VANISHING POINT
A CLONE WARS ADVENTURE
MYGEETO.

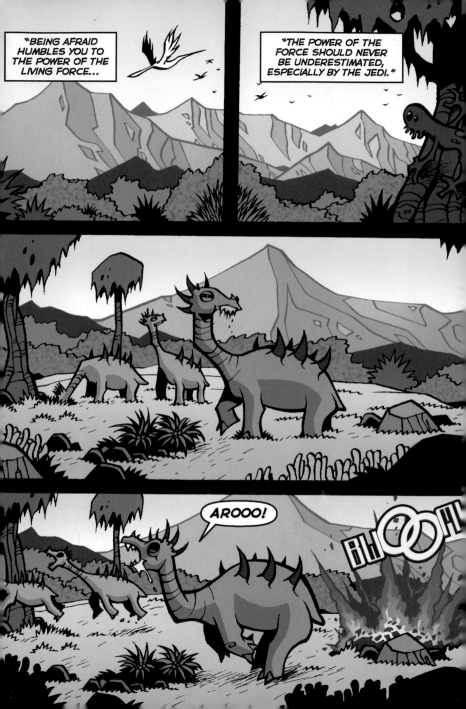

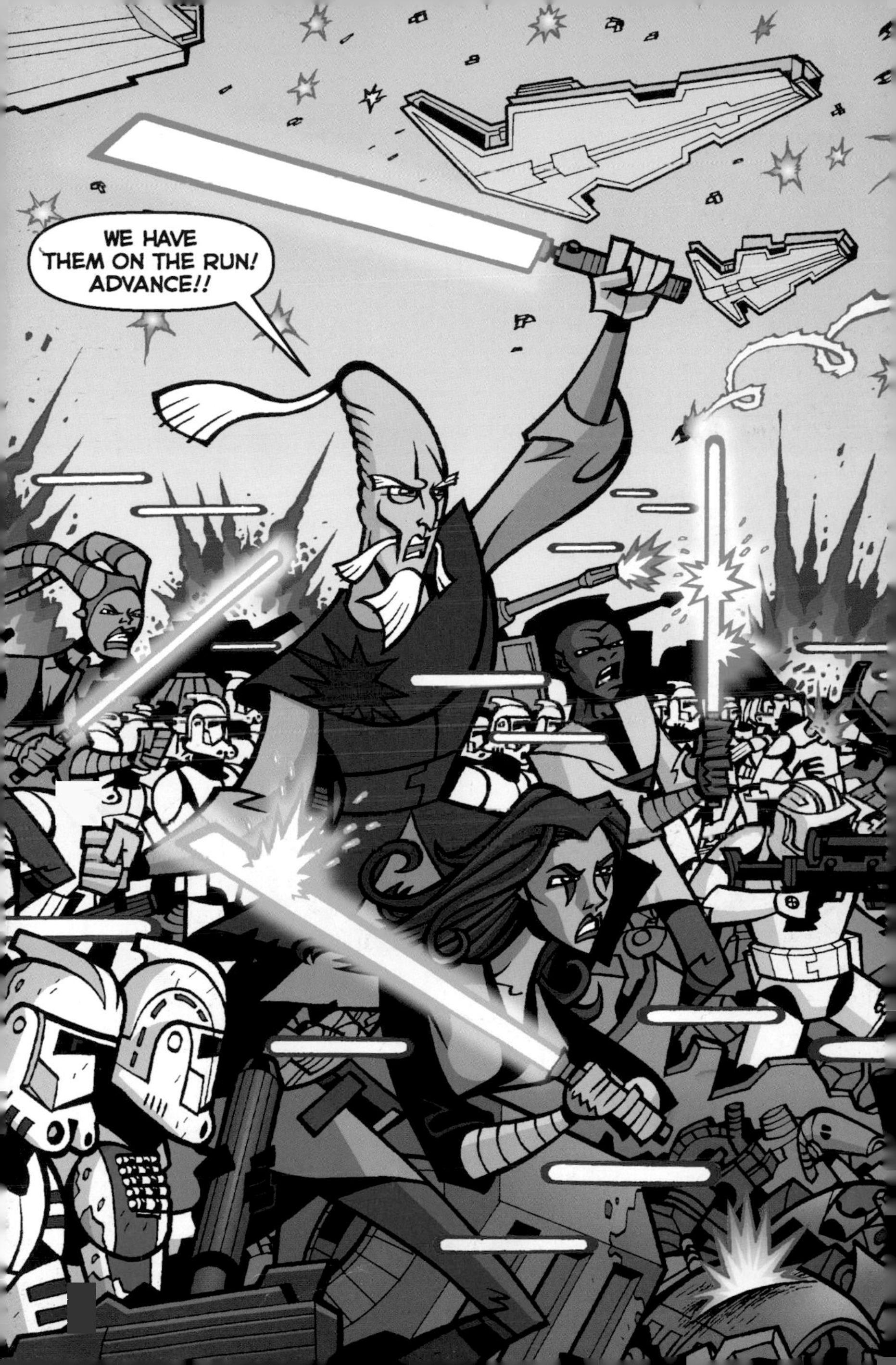
WE HAVE THEM ON THE RUN! ADVANCE!!

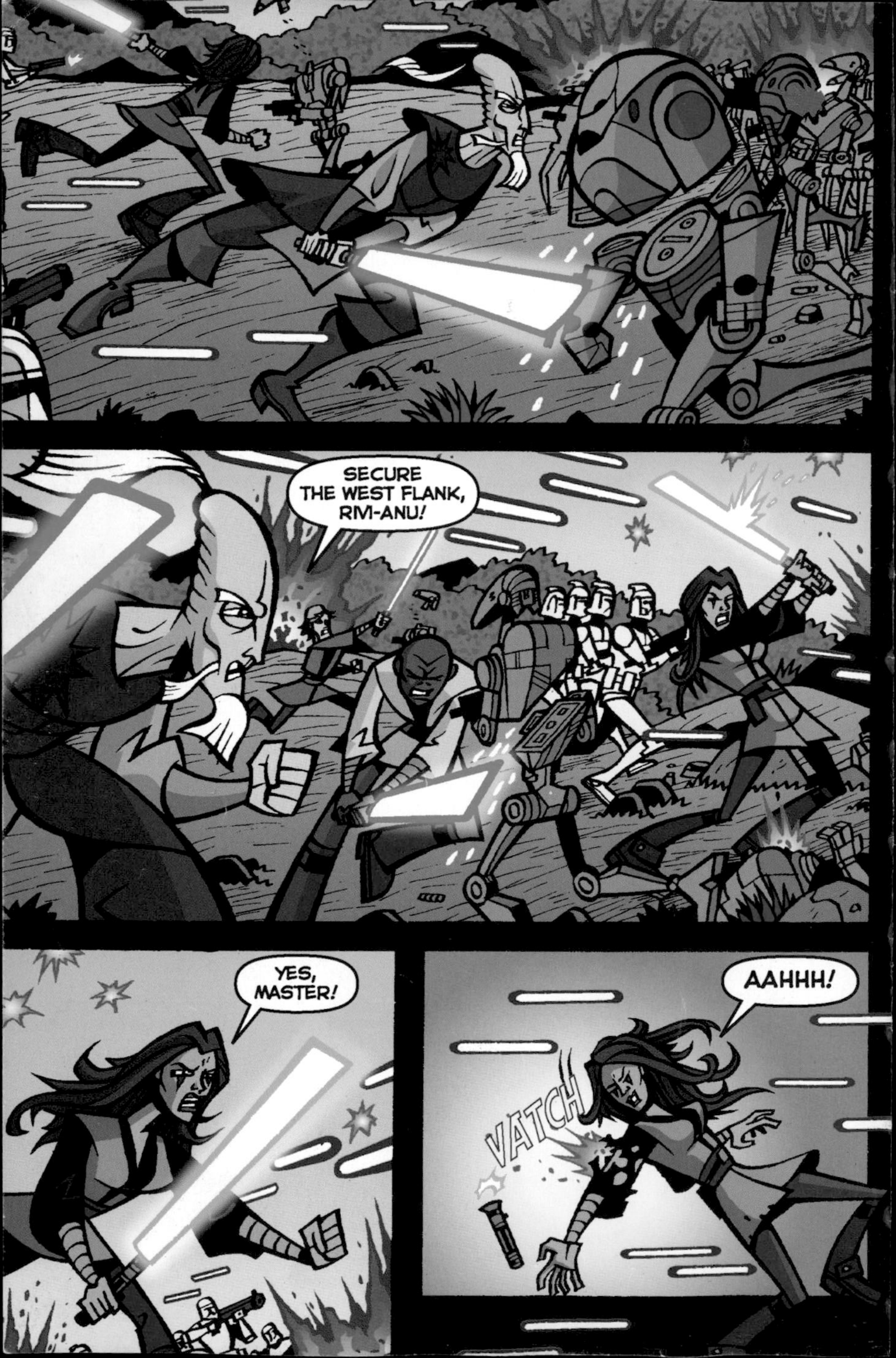
SECURE THE WEST FLANK, RM-ANU!
YES, MASTER!
AAHHH!
VATCH

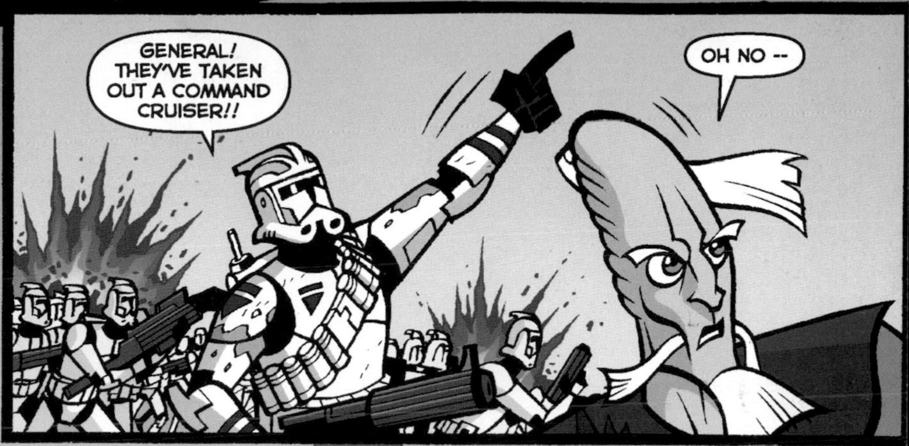
GENERAL! THEY'VE TAKEN OUT A COMMAND CRUISER!!
OH NO --

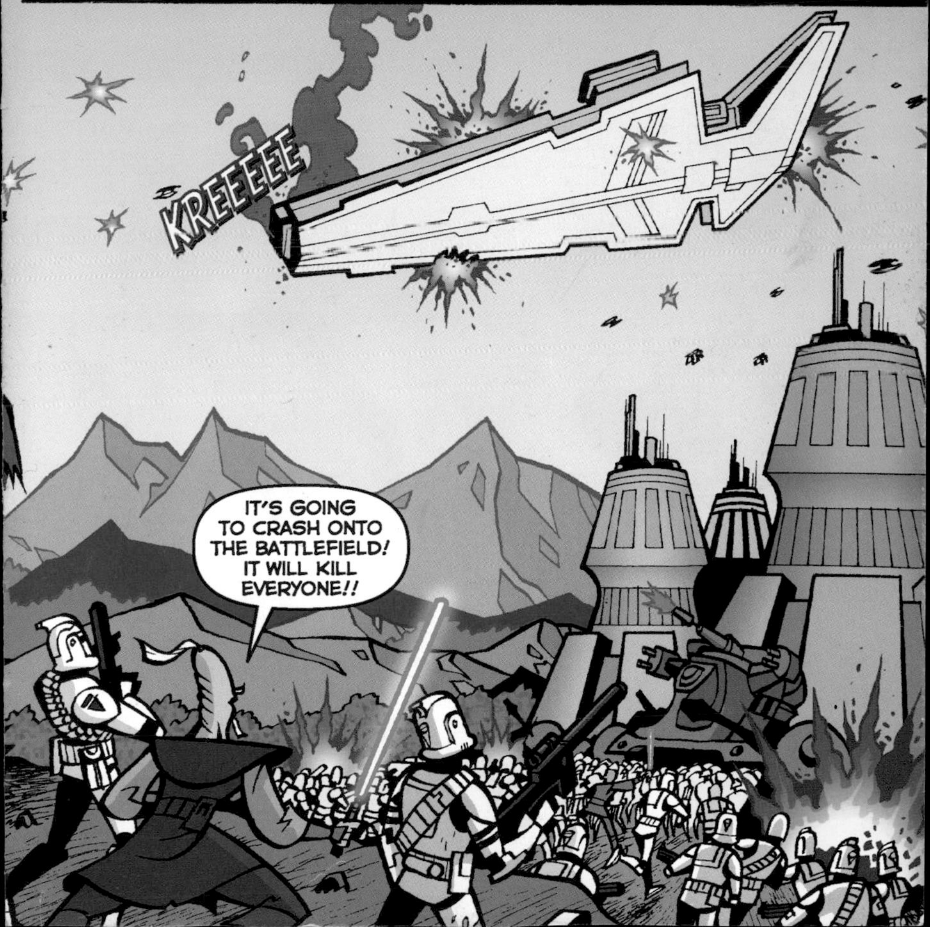
KREEEEE
IT'S GOING TO CRASH ONTO THE BATTLEFIELD! IT WILL KILL EVERYONE!!

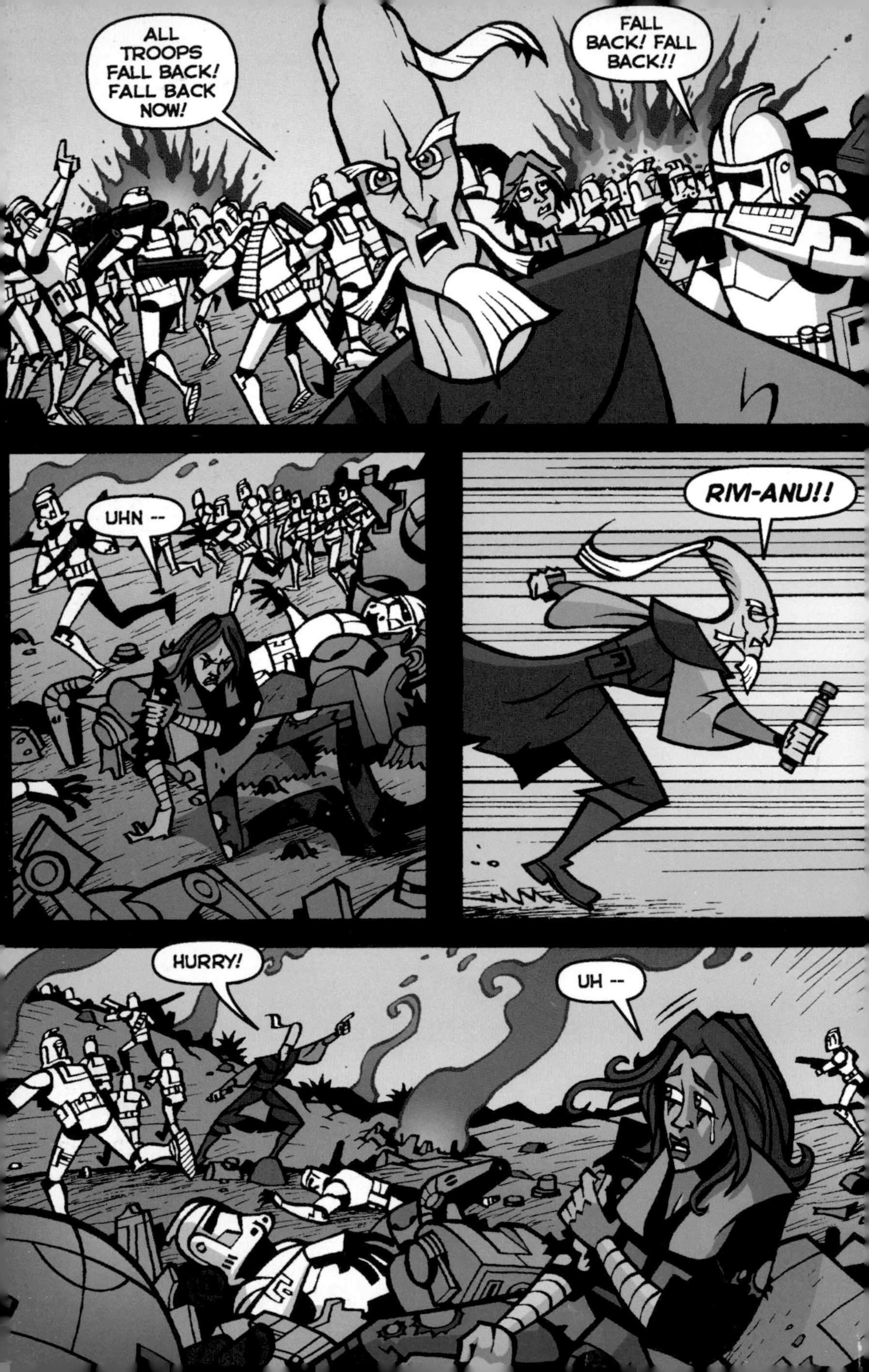
ALL TROOPS FALL BACK! FALL BACK NOW!
FALL BACK! FALL BACK!!
UHN --
RIVI-ANU!!
HURRY!
UH --

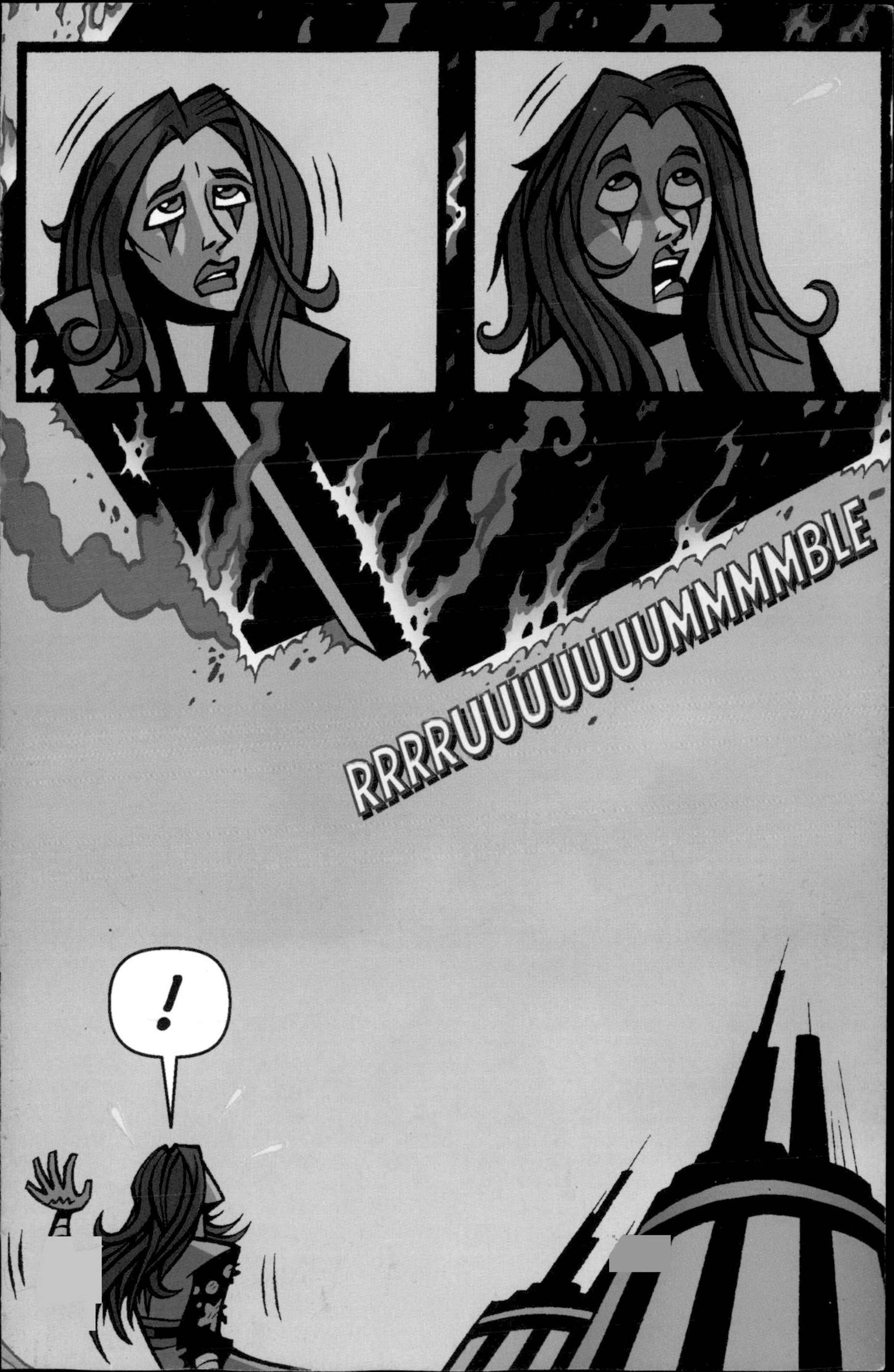
RRRRUUUUUUUUMMMMMBLE
!

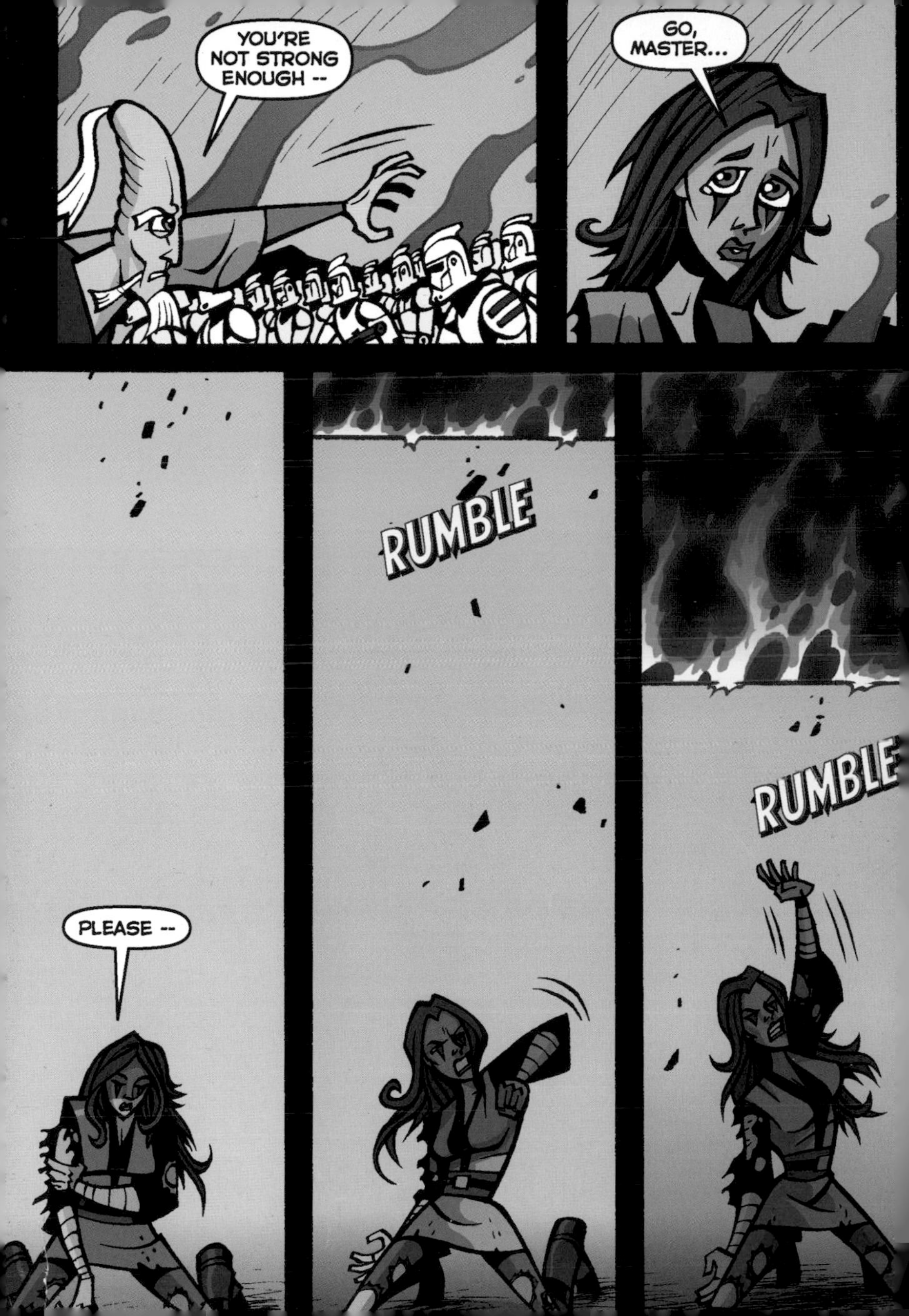
YOU'RE NOT STRONG ENOUGH --
GO, MASTER...
PLEASE --
RUMBLE
RUMBLE

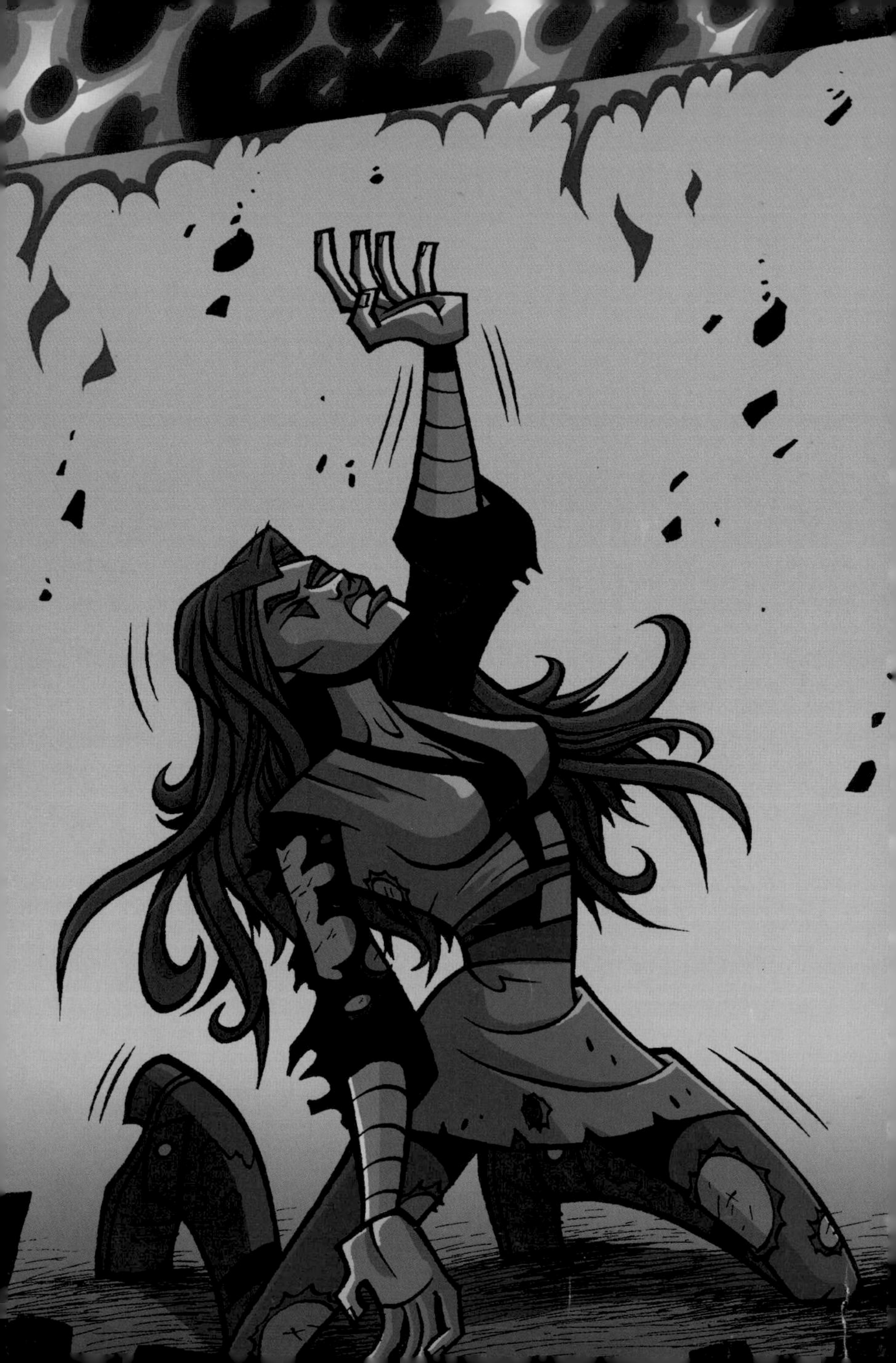

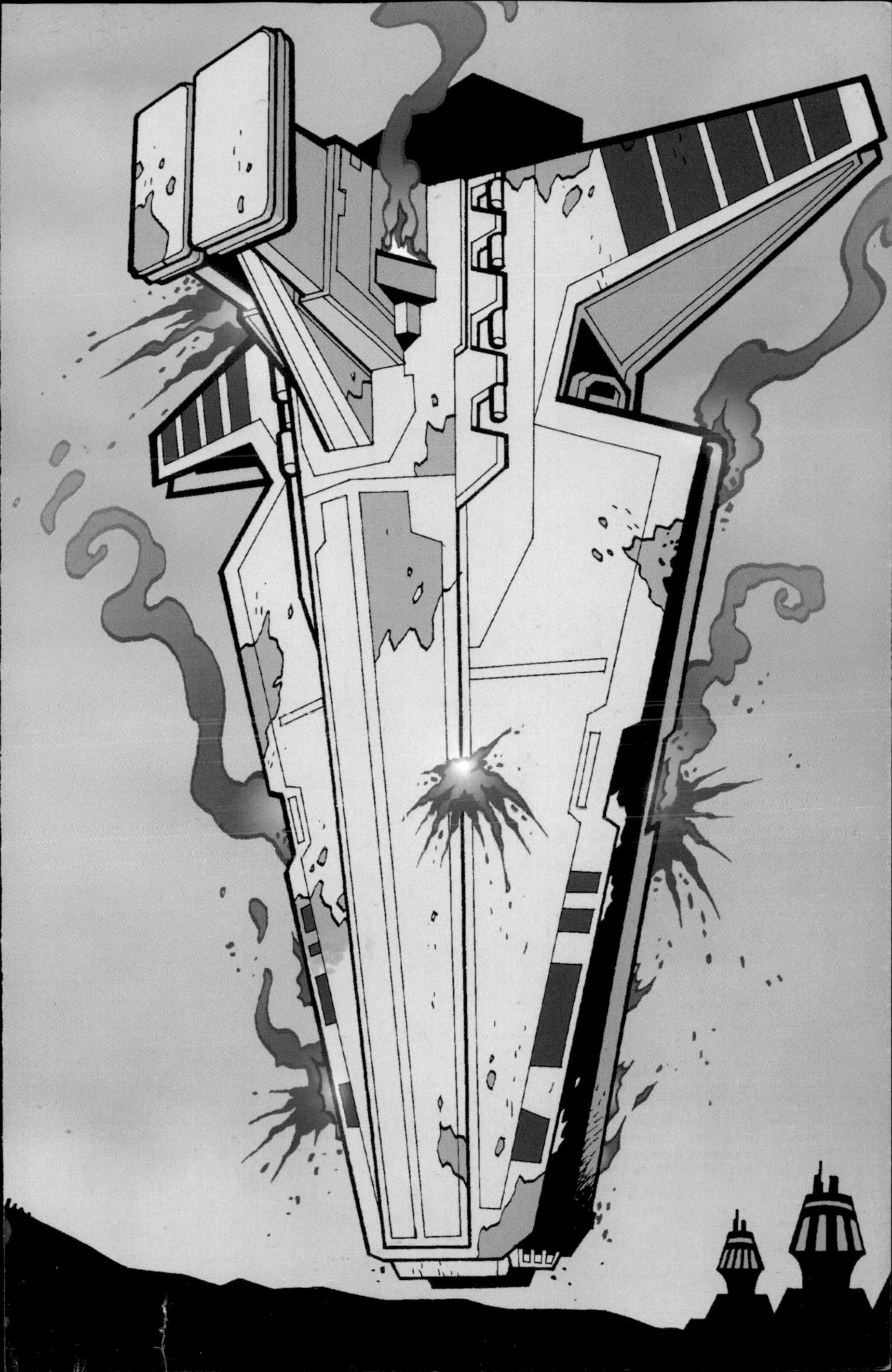

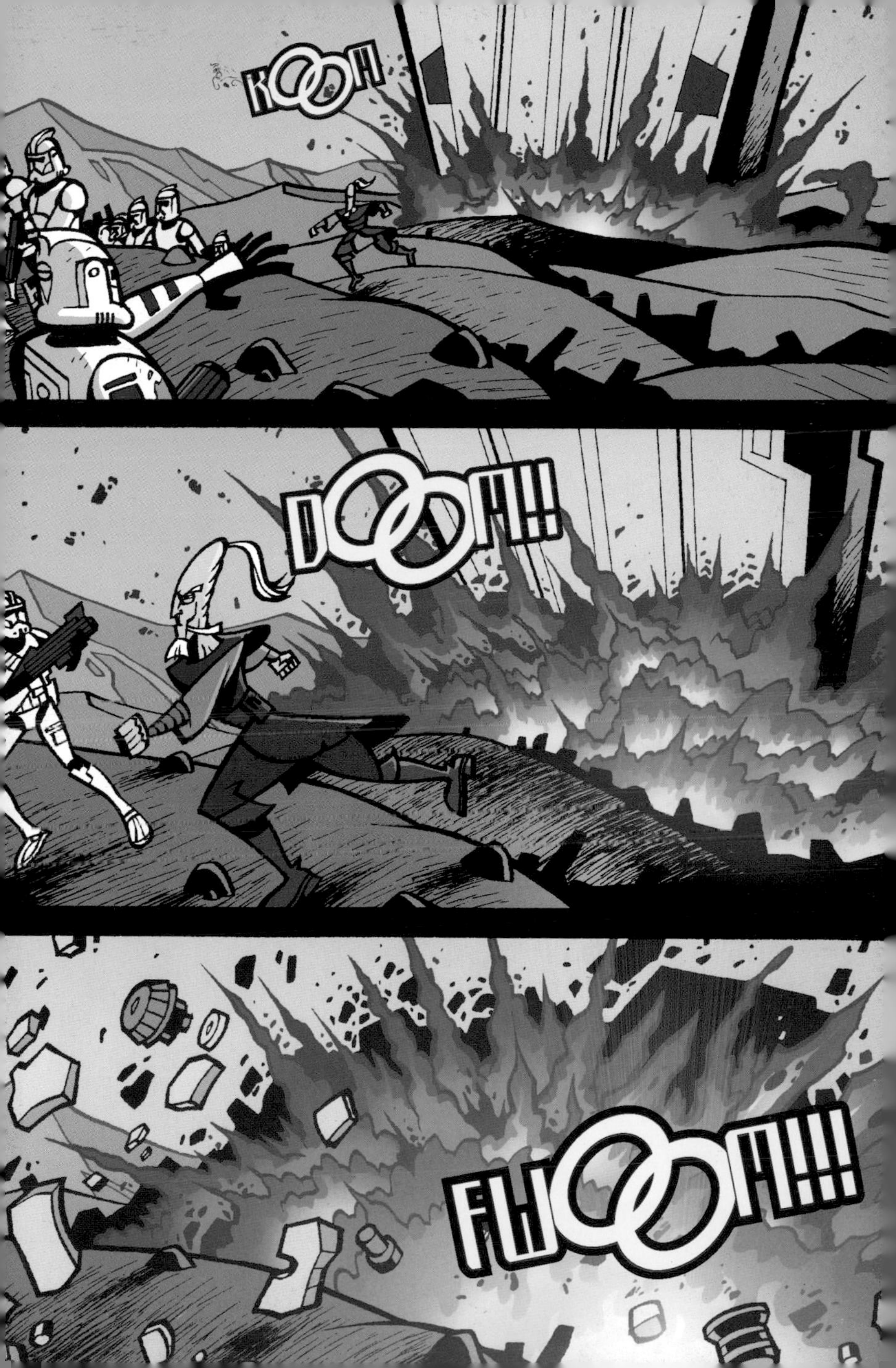
KOOM
DOOM!!
FWOOM!!!

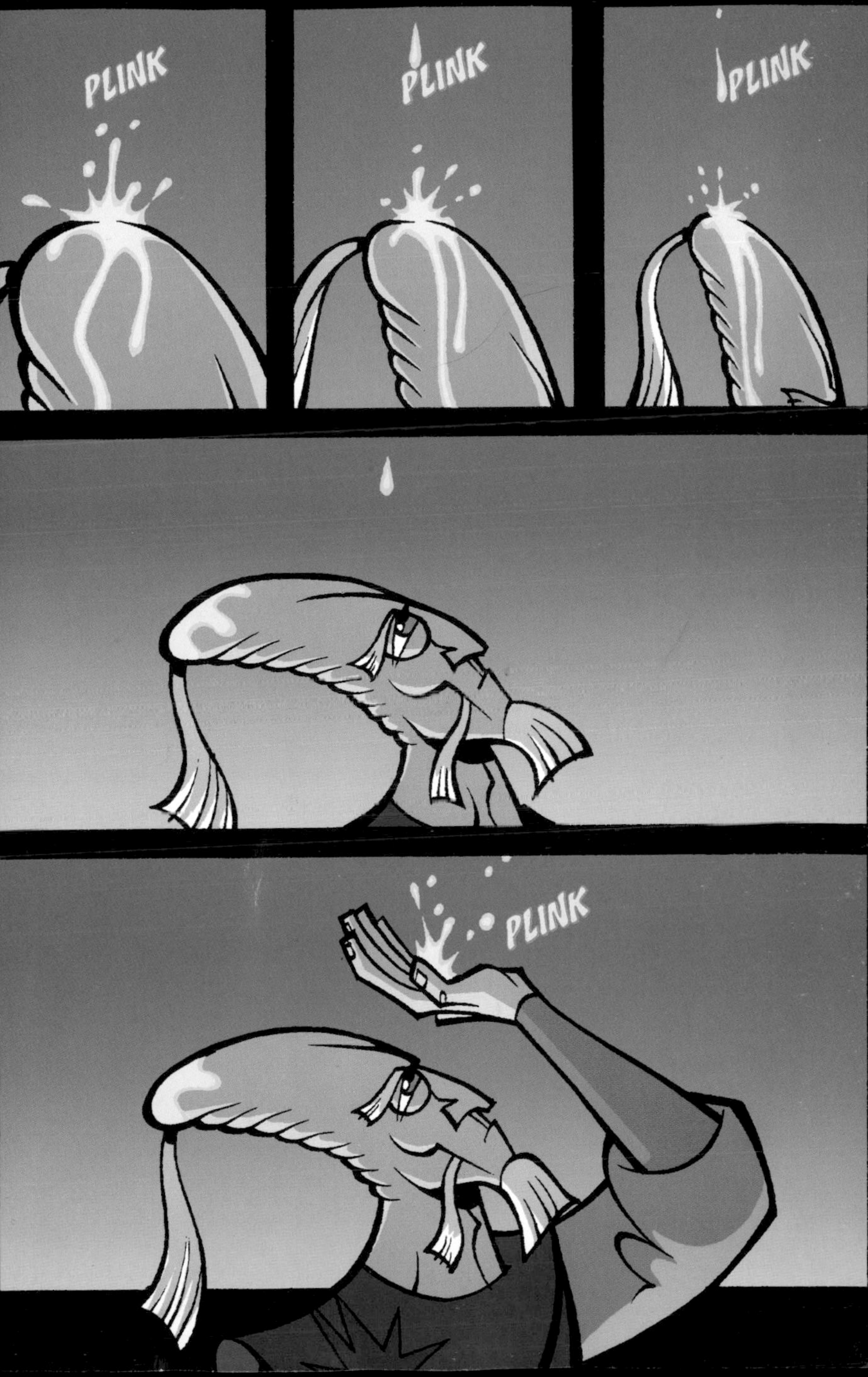
PLINK
PLINK
PLINK
PLINK

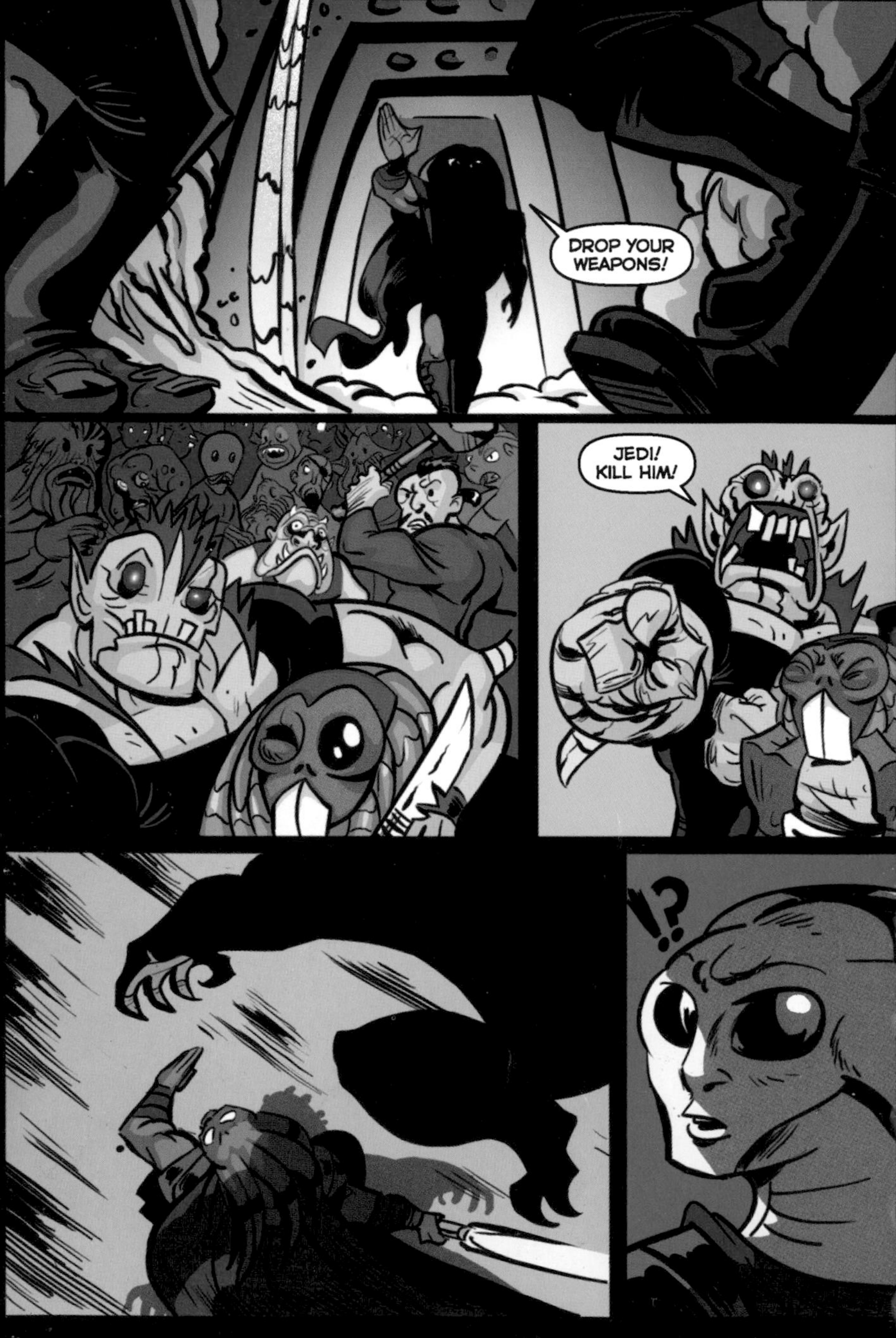
DROP YOUR WEAPONS!
JEDI! KILL HIM!
!?

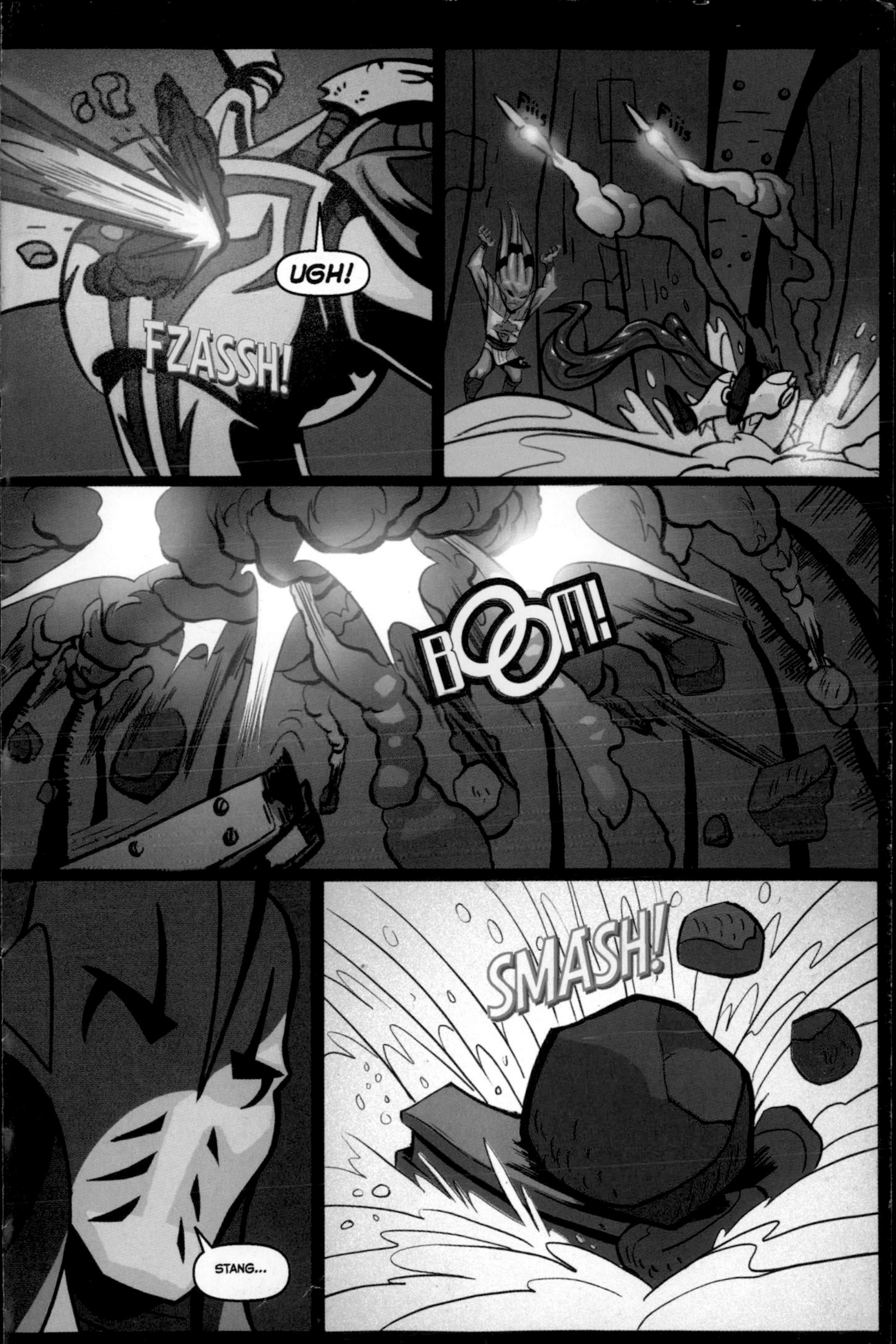
UGH!
FZASSH!
Fiiis
Fiiis
BOOM!
SMASH!
STANG...

CLONE WARS ADVENTURES

Don't miss any of the action-packed adventures of your favorite **STAR WARS**® characters, availble at comics shops and bookstores in a galaxy near you!

Volume 1
ISBN: 1-59307-243-0 / $6.95

Volume 2
ISBN: 1-59307-271-6 / $6.95

Volume 3
ISBN: 1-59307-307-0 / $6.95

Volume 4
ISBN: 1-59307-402-6 / $6.95

STAR WARS® CLONE WARS

Experience all the excitement and drama of the Clone Wars! Look for these trade paperbacks at a comics shop or book store near you!

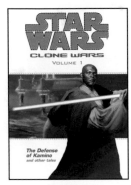

Volume 1
ISBN: 1-56971-962-4 / $14.95

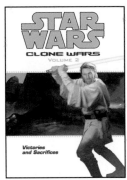

Volume 2
ISBN: 1-56971-969-1 / $14.95

Volume 3
ISBN: 1-59307-006-3 / $14.95

Volume 4
ISBN: 1-59307-195-7 / $16.95

ALSO AVAILABLE

Volume 5
ISBN: 1-59307-273-2 / $14.95

Volume 6
ISBN: 1-59307-352-6 / $17.95